NIGHT LIFE

www.penguin.co.uk

Night Life

Exploring Britain's Wild
Landscapes After Dark

John Lewis-Stempel

doubleday

TRANSWORLD PUBLISHERS

UK | USA | Canada | Ireland | Australia
India | New Zealand | South Africa

Transworld is part of the Penguin Random House group of companies
whose addresses can be found at global.penguinrandomhouse.com.

Penguin Random House UK, One Embassy Gardens,
8 Viaduct Gardens, London SW11 7BW

penguin.co.uk

Penguin
Random House
UK

First published in Great Britain in 2025 by Doubleday
an imprint of Transworld Publishers

003

Typeset in 11/14.5 pt Goudy Oldstyle Std by
Six Red Marbles UK, Thetford, Norfolk
Printed and bound in Great Britain by Clays Ltd, Elcograf S.p.A.

The authorized representative in the EEA is Penguin Random House Ireland,
Morrison Chambers, 32 Nassau Street, Dublin D02 YH68.

A CIP catalogue record for this book is available from the British Library.

ISBN 9781529938159

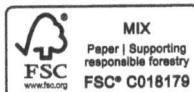

To Tris, Freda and Penny.
The night belongs to those who love it.
You.

Contents

The Starlight Night

Look at the stars! look, look up at the skies!
  O look at all the fire-folk sitting in the air!
  The bright boroughs, the circle-citadels there!
Down in dim woods the diamond delves! the elves'-eyes!
The grey lawns cold where gold, where quickgold lies!
  Wind-beat whitebeam! airy abeles set on a flare!
  Flake-doves sent floating forth at a farmyard scare!
Ah well! it is all a purchase, all is a prize.

Buy then! bid then! – What? – Prayer, patience, alms,
  vows.
Look, look: a May-mess, like on orchard boughs!
  Look! March-bloom, like on mealed-with-yellow
  sallows!
These are indeed the barn; withindoors house
The shocks. This piece-bright paling shuts the spouse
  Christ home, Christ and his mother and all his hallows.

Gerard Manley Hopkins

INTRODUCTION

Fear and Loving of the Night

Jesu Lord, blyssed thou be,
For all this nyght thou hast me kepe
From the f[i]end and his poste,
Whether I wake or that I slepe.

THE RELIEF OF the medieval prayer-writer on see-ing dawn is evident down the centuries. The uncertainties and phantasmagoria of the dark hours banished, done; the sanctuary of a brand-new day revealed by rosy-fingered dawn.

Achluophobia, lygophobia, nyctophobia, scoto-phobia – whatever you call it, fear of the dark night is as old as humanity. It is natural, an innate trepida-tion that stems from the time of the prehistoric mists when we were not, courtesy of technology, the apex predator that we are today. Humans rely primarily on the sense of sight, which is disadvantaged in darkness. Indeed, we are doubly disadvantaged since what night

1

vision we do have is relatively poor – unlike that of the big cats that prowl the African savannah.

Our fear of the night is an evolutionary survival trait. Ancestors who failed to stay safe in the deep, nocturnal hours died. Over the millennia, the nocturnal world became the repository of anxieties, which were rendered into personifications or supernatural/ unnatural beings. In Greek mythology the goddess Nyx, wearing a star-studded black robe, emerged from a cave to ride across the sky in a chariot pulled by black steeds. She was Night, and she was Death. The night, in the human mind, became the abode of sprites, goblins, witches and monsters. For years, according to the Anglo-Saxon poem *Beowulf*, the ravening creature Grendel attacked the mead hall of Heorot, and consumed men unlucky enough to fall into his claws. Fear of the dark is fear of the unknown.

The Enlightenment and the streetlamps of contemporary civilization have all but banished fear of supernatural beings in the West. Few believe in sprites and elves any more. But the lights of the modern world have obliterated any meaningful connection to the night. We have lost touch with its wonders as well as its terrors. The Ancients may have fretted about malevolent spirits abroad in the dark, but did not gazing up at the stars cause them to think big, about God, the workings of the universe, what it is to be human? For many today the natural night is truly the unknown.

It is the farmer-naturalist's luck to work mainly outdoors and for long hours. And frequently into the dark hours.

Like I did last night, a May night of a waxing moon and sweet with the scent of naked warm earth, greening grass, and spiced by the phosphorescent hawthorn blossom. I was late feeding the pigs, who do not like to be kept waiting at dinner time, and I had driven the tractor full throttle down to the wood, a sack of sow nuts and a Labrador sliding about in the metal transport box on the back. As I heaved the sack out of the box my peripheral vision remarked three hares 'boxing' in the field next door, where the moonlight gleamed on the freshly tilled soil. Spring moonlight has a different quality to winter moonlight; the night sky has unhardened, and the lunar beams are as gentle as caresses.

Prosaically, the boxing of hares is an unreceptive female fending off ardent males. Jill versus Jacks, a battle of the sexes. But hares at night always twist the scene, make the ordinary extraordinary. Such was the angle of the land that against the moon the hares were silhouettes, and up on their back legs the animals, with their flurrying arms, became human dancers. One hare slumped down into an earthen clump, a sod, only to rise from the earth, born again. The night hares were brazen, their daylight timidities thrown away. I cannot tell you if they made noise in their pugilism; the purring of the tractor blanked all other sound. I was a spectator to a mime.

Watching the contorting hares, I understood why the people of the past likened boxing hares to a coven of tiny dancing witches. Or considered them, as partly nocturnal creatures, as belonging to the moon. I looked up that night and beheld the moon and saw, as people all over the world do, shadow-patterns in the shape of a hare. In Celtic myth Eostre changed shape to become a hare at the full moon; all hares were sacred to her and acted as her messengers. Small wonder, perhaps, that the Celts were so opposed to eating hare. Since hares, however, were heavenly messengers, it made sense – to the Celts – that they could be used as instruments of divination, by studying the patterns of their tracks, the rituals of their mating dances and details within their entrails.

These were some of my wonderings and recollections as I gazed at the trio of hares. The dog was less entranced and barked. The three hares evanesced, as fast as terror, as though they had never been. A witchy trick.

You will have got the point. The real creatures of the night are fabulously interesting, and the night allows imagining in a way that the 'cold light of day' does not. At night the senses become reordered – hearing becomes privileged over vision – an alteration to the human being that makes one more 'animal', more sensitive to nature.

This is my second book of nightwalks, a sequel to *Nightwalking*. Once again, I can be found in my natural habitat, the farmland of England. But here I also wander further afield, to terrains new. In every place, I have tried to show why the night is precious, and what it is to be human in the dark.

Owl-light

Come out and hear the owls shout
In the still and dewy night-hour;
The moon a fading white flower
Hangs low, with mists about.
Like pale moths, along the hedge
Withering bindweed lies;
Night looks in with hollow eyes,
Dim at the window-ledge.
With weird shriek, the hunting bird
Flits sorrowfully by;
Mournful woods against the sky
Are full of griefs unheard.
Trancèd scents of dying flowers
In Summer's requiem wreath;
Not a breath – but damp of death,
And sea tolling the hours.

Rose Arresti

Part I

Silent Night

MIDNIGHT, IN THE midnight of the year. We were late back from the carol service, and the inevitable post-event mince pies and wine. But I could not go to bed. There were sheep to be checked. In my ears, of course, hummed the words of Nahum Tate's 'While shepherds watched their flocks by night'. In Christ-time shepherds on the night-watch were seated on the ground; in the winters of medieval Britain shepherds crouched in convenient, weather-proof shrubbery (hence 'Shepherd's Bush'); the modern English shepherd in December tends to haul him or herself off the sofa for a quick night-time check of their charges. The principle of watchful care remains the same, however. Shepherding is eternal. Anyway, at midnight I put on a headtorch, the Barbour, went outside, grimaced at the cold, went back into the hall, put a gilet on top of the Barbour. It was two-coat cold. Only a single dog, my Labrador Plum, could be budged from in front of the fire; but then she is my shadow.

The starshine and the moonshine were sufficient to see the black dog excited to accompany the master on his rounds, and that Frost had commenced his white embrace. Under the vast dome of the silent starred sky I took the familiar track up to the sheep; a barn owl hunted the wheat field, in long systematic traverses, as if following the ploughman's lengths. There was pattern also in the bird's wing motion, a few rapid beats, then a long glide on rigid wings; a time-wrought avian algorithm. When it banked to turn, the white of its breast was blinding, and for a flash-second there were two moons in the sky. The barn owl in the horse field usurped the previous and aged *Tyto alba* holder of the fiefdom a month back. I hailed the new owl-king.

The further up the track, the closer and more tantalizing were the stars. I could have plucked them and packed the pockets of my coats with their jewels. Somewhere in the trees down by the brook, a vixen screamed for a mate; the sound, one of the saddest in the world, stone-skipped down the hard earth of frosted valley into nothingness. Midwinter is the main mating time for the foxes, but no dog fox answered her call.

The domestic dog and I hurried on and reached the sheep in their paddock; to the west there was only

darkness and far away in the east the city lights floated in the blackness.

I had a headtorch, but there was no need for it to see, under the starshine and the moonshine, the sheep on the pearly grass; the flock stood warily, and one or two ewes lowered their rears for the pee that precedes potential flight. They then recognized their shepherd and his dog and flopped back down on the ground. The starlight settled on their backs, spinning a white corona around every one of them. The ewes were in lamb, and their contentment came off them like heat.

Duty done, I decided to extend our walk; well, the night was heavenly. I cut across the meadow, deep and crisp with frost, and as true and white and even as snow. Under my boots the frost creaked; the dog and I seemed a scene observed from the outside, a line drawing from the Victorian era: 'Shepherd and Dog on a Winter's Night'. We entered the oak wood. From somewhere unseen came the sharp snapping of fallen branches under deer hooves; then I saw them, dim archaic shapes, moving parallel. One raised its head, scenting – then fled, the troop turning as one fluid motion into the arboreal depth, white rumps flashing, like naval signal lamps at sea.

The wood returned to its winter quiet, which, in the freezing night, was absolute aside from the scratching of shrews among the iced fallen oak leaves. Poor shrews, condemned never to hibernate, always to eat, whatever the weather; a touching, tender tragedy.

I shrank further down into my coats. We were out of the wood, just into the long meadow, when the dog stopped dead, hackles raised, and I almost fell over

her: fifty yards away, a grey dog fox crossed our path. Either it failed to see us, or it imperiously ignored us (and I fancy the latter), and it stuck to its course, nose in the air, until it was swallowed in the black hole of the hedge. Perhaps the vixen would be a lonely heart no longer.

In midwinter, like midsummer, the night seems enchanted, on the oneiric cusp of another dimension. The very air charged with magic. I had been walking with the moon at my back; when I turned for home, the moon had been appointed with a perfect holy halo. The explanation for a moon ring is prosaic, being moonlight refracted through ice crystals in high cloud. The sight of one is divine.

By now the dog and I had been out for nearly forty minutes, so we headed back to our den. I had seen the stars, a barn owl, a fox and a lunar halo. These were the delights of a lowly shepherd's walk in the night in winter.

It was one of those December silent nights when the air is pure and glass-hard. Although the slow-rising moon was enmeshed by the scrawny branches of the hedge, the land was lit by a million stars; the gently rolling fields were silver-plated to the horizon. The black dog's back sheened with starshine, and the

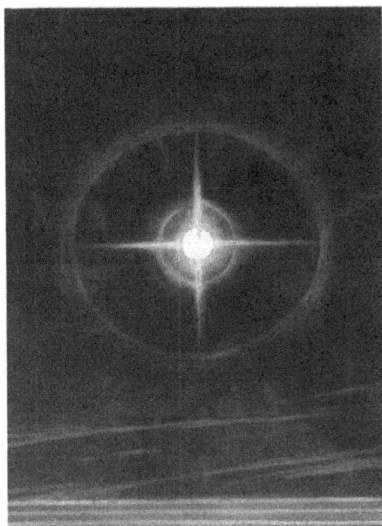

night's quiet was broken only by the sound of my squealing wheelbarrow as I pushed it up the lane, and the *kerwick*-ing of a tawny owl down in the trees by the horse field.

In my years of being star-struck I've never seen a red-nosed reindeer in the December night, but it produces prodigies nonetheless: the south sky streaked with shooting stars as prolific as Stalin's Katyusha rockets. They blazed out of the constellation Gemini at the rate of one a minute. Whereas most meteor showers are composed of comets, the Geminids, a

December phenomenon first observed by the Royal Observatory in 1862, are caused by debris from an asteroid entering Earth's atmosphere at speeds to up to 150,000mph. The Geminids are a multi-coloured light show. Elements of sodium and calcium found within the celestial debris cause it to glow white, red, green, yellow or blue on vaporization.

December. 'Tis the month for shooting stars, with the Ursids delivering their five to ten meteors per hour too.

Shooting stars in the dark night sky. Seconds of individual brilliance, like the fading tracks of radioactive particles in a cloud chamber. Since even the stars burn out in the end.

My star-gazing and musing left the dog cold; ahead of me, she turned and barked to remind me of my proper purpose. We went on, Sirius our steering star; the cows were where they should be, slumbered on the high ground.

As a son of the country, I do not care to be without holly at Christmas, its sprigs popped behind paintings on walls, a single sprig propped in the centre of the brandy-flamed pudding. I cut the holly for decoration yesterday evening, from a lone tree in the centre of the wood, a location secret and too obscure for the invading, berry-gobbling host of Viking birds,

the redwings and fieldfares. But in the time of gifts, do
not the farmyard animals deserve their presents too?
Bunches of holly always make interesting eating for
cattle in winter, when their diet is hay, and more hay,
which is dried grass upon dried grass. Holly is tonic
too, rich in protein and nutrients. The nation's agriculturalists knew this once.

With gloved hands I spread the holly along the
base of the wire stock fence, and the four cows raised
their great bodies, and plodded, puffing, to their gift.

The beeves masticated the thick, luscious leaves of holly slowly, and gazed into the far distance as if pondering arcane and ancient Christmas mysteries of which I, a poor human, was ignorant.

Down at the bottom of the field, I was not surprised to see the fox, or indeed the badger; like us, the animals have their routines, their familiar well-trodden pathways. Indeed, the fox and the badger headed towards each other on the same convenient causeway, this dinted into the ground by the passing years of passing cattle and sheep. (The wild things utilizing agriculture: a proof, which I was unable to resist, for my own scripture of organic farming.) The Reverend Gilbert White, he of Selborne and the pro-creator of British nature-writing, once remarked, 'A good ornithologist should be able to distinguish birds by their air as well as by their colors and shape.' The same goes for the mammal-spotter. The grey-backed badger was nearly camouflaged by the starshine; it was the bear-shambling confidence that caught the eye and identified the creature as Brock. It was the alert trotting that gave Renard, nearer to the swallowing black shadow of the hedge, away. (Foxes almost always trot and never walk.) I conjectured which of the two, in their head-on meeting, would give way; but perfect wise gentlemen, they stepped aside for each other.

I watched to see which way they would go; the fox slunk under the gate on to the road, doubtless after car-slayed carrion. The badger squatted and scented, then headed up the field towards the dog and me. My silhouette, a long man painted black on the hillside, motioned at the dog to sit. Badgers do not properly hibernate; they only enter the zombie state in days endless with snow, hoar frost. They remain active on the poorest pickings, such as slugs, acorns and dog-mercury root; palaeontological evidence shows that badgers have inhabited the British Isles for at least 250,000 years, so you would expect them to have learned to make do. Badgers do, though, have a definite taste for the red meat of earthworms, such as *Eisenia fetida* and *Dendrobaena veneta* found in a muck-heap. And there was a massive muck-heap directly behind us.

The boar badger bumbled upwards until I could see the glisten of star rays on his wet snout. Nature is not always as acutely alert as we divorced humans believe. Or as elegant. *Meles meles* is an ungainly runner – at speed, on the retreat, such as on sighting a man and his dog a yard away, its rump looks like a plump man in baggy trousers. Still, the animal can achieve a creditable 19mph gallop. I aver, downhill, heading for its sett, it might go even faster.

Again, the dog and I returned home via the wood, where the tawny owls were performing their own car-olling amid the stark trees. Hooting. *Tu-whoo*ing. However transliterated, these are love songs, war songs, chansons for finding for mates, declaring possession. Like the noun 'owl', the aural descriptors are associative with the howl of the wolf, another night creature. A tawny can be summoned. The Reverend C. A. Johns, another of those parson naturalists that England once bred in profusion, instructed readers of *British Birds in Their Haunts*, 1909, that the territorial *woo* of the owl may be imitated exactly by forming a hollow with the fingers and the palms of two hands, leaving an opening only between the second joints of the two thumbs, and then by blowing with considerable force down upon the opening thus made, so as to produce the sound *hoo-hoo-hoo-h-o-o-o*.

I did it, and an owl called back. A hoot, in the jocular sense, also humbling in a real sense: a connection across species, a confirmation of acceptance in nature. But I was a wise owl, myself. A male tawny who has failed to establish a personal fiefdom territory by late winter, either by superior fighting or calling, is a tawny doomed. To maintain territory tawnies will attack trespassing owls – and even foxes, dogs, not to mention humans. Eric Hosking, the famous photographer of birds, lost an eye in a tawny attack. He titled his autobiography *An Eye for a Bird*.

Night Notes: The Sound of Silence

Silence comes in many forms. There is the nothingness silence of the grave, a type of void; and there is
the silence of Holy Night, Silent Night, the restful
stillness you encounter on leaving a country church
after midnight mass. The vast silence of the winter
shore on a grey, lassitudinous February day is a lesson
in human insignificance.

Animals understand the need for silence whether
predator or prey, particularly the animals of the night:
the owl flies on silent wings and the fox pads softly
on muffling, furred feet. The wounded sheep will not
bleat, because to do so would betray its state to the
wolf; there may be no wolves in Britain, but ancestral
fear retains its imprimatur.

So requisite, primal, is the human need for silence
that we construct physical spaces in which to hear it.
The monks had their cloisters, cathedrals their chapel
of rest, and Virgina Woolf was famously eloquent on
the need for female writers to have a 'room of one's
own'. No one ever built a walled garden without desir-
ing the banishment of exterior noise. And silence in
the library, please! And no phones in the 'quiet car-
riage' of the InterCity.

When we speak of silence in nature, we mean,

contrarily, that we wish to hear the natural acoustic system. We seek escape from 'anthropogenic' noise, we seek silence from invasive, mechanical modern life, with its iPhone beep, cacophonic traffic on the city ring road, airplane scrape across the sky. And from the chatter of humans, the madding crowd. It is no small accident that our greatest nature writers sought solitude. Wordsworth, famously, wandered as lonely as cloud, while fellow Romantic poet John Clare, after complaining that 'I hate the very noise of troublous man', declared:

> There is a charm in Solitude that cheers
> A feeling that the world knows nothing of
> A green delight the wounded mind endears
> After the hustling world is broken off . . .

The great philosopher of nature's quiet and its benefit to man was the American woodsman Henry David Thoreau, he of Walden Pond:

> Silence is the universal refuge, the sequel to all dull discourses and all foolish acts, a balm to our every chagrin, as welcome after satiety as after disappointment; that background which the painter may not daub, be he master or bungler, and which, however awkward a figure

we may have made in the foreground, remains ever our
inviolable asylum, where no indignity can assail, no per-
sonality disturb us.

In silence, we are. Monastic orders necessarily observe precepts of non-talking, just as Mahatma
Gandhi deliberately chose dumbness one day a week.
Humans: they will talk, won't they? Even on a ramble
to listen to nature, someone cannot resist saying, 'Did
you hear that?' People sometimes fill their lives with
distracting noise in order to not be.

Only when one understands that the search for
silence is also the seeking of solitude (or sympathetic,
mute-mouthed companionship) can one find the true
quiet of nature. In nature, there is no actual silence,
other than death, which we have unhappily inflicted
on the chemically doused fields of industrialized food
production. Rachel Carson's 1962 book of environ-
mental science, *Silent Spring*, is their appositely titled
requiem.

If one escapes anthropogenic noise, the subtle
sounds of nature are curiously amplified: the rustle
of the zephyr in the restless reeds can fill a Norfolk
Broad. They are also particular. Each landscape is a
soundscape, with its own acoustic ecology. The hills
have their eagle screams, the coast its cliffs of crying

seabirds, the lake the *plop* of trout returning to their element on discovering that they cannot, after all, fly.

Quiet, or silence if you will, is more than a question of place, or human agency. Weather and time are also hush-makers. Snow is nature's great damper of sound. Under a 'blanket' of snow even cities can be stilled, and the sense of antiquity that snow brings with it – a dusting of snow makes even the modern skyscraper look olde – only improves the feeling of serenity. Fog, too, is a bringer of quietude, ordering airplanes to ground. Winter sends the world to sleep; the wood in winter is as hushed as a temple, in contrast to May, when it resounds to birdsong and picnickers. And so we come to the night, the great, dark continent of quiet. Just as he was the prophet of silence, so was Thoreau the prophet of the night, for they were overlapping entities. In his journal in 1853 he declared, 'I wish to hear the silence of the night, for the silence is something positive and to be heard.'

The night is always home to the seekers of silence. Blaring humans are tucked up in their beds, their restless cars finally fixed on the drive. Night is the realm where nature's quiet still holds sway. And, happily, at night we reorder our senses. Hearing is prioritized over sight. Those who walk at night truly enjoy, with their alerted hearing, the sounds of silence, from the natural acoustic of particular place to the hum of the universe, and all of them balm.

The secret of course is to be silent oneself, like the fox and the owl. Silence is as silence does.

Out in the Dark

Out in the dark over the snow
The fallow fawns invisible go
With the fallow doe;
And the winds blow
Fast as the stars are slow.

Stealthily the dark haunts round
And, when the lamp goes, without sound
At a swifter bound
Than the swiftest hound,
Arrives, and all else is drowned;

And star and I and wind and deer,
Are in the dark together, – near,
Yet far, – and fear
Drums on my ear
In that sage company drear.

How weak and little is the light,
All the universe of sight,
Love and delight,
Before the might,
If you love it not, of night.

Edward Thomas

29

Part II

Wandering Lonely

It is the loneliest place of all these hills

William Wordsworth on Kidsty Pike,
Haweswater (*The Brothers*, 1880)

HAWESWATER, THE EASTERN-MOST water body of the
Lake District, is a liquid black hole on Earth. We
arrived late on a March night, along the single-track
road, and were not well met by moonlight, or even
much light at all. It was a drive into a void, despite
being a mere twenty minutes from the M6 motorway.

Haweswater: it is a place of paradox. At 807 feet
above sea level it is water suspended in the sky. Offi-
cially a reservoir, it subsumes the natural lakelets of
High Water and Low Water; between 1936 and 1941
the Manchester Corporation built Haweswater Dam,
flooding the valley – the water level rose by some

90 feet – to create a mountain-limned length of liquid four miles long and half a mile wide. The damming was to create a water supply for the people of the northwest's industrial centres, so that they might not die of thirst; lost beneath the flood were the pretty, centuries-old villages of Measand and Mardale Green, demised by drowning. For city life, country death. An old tale.

Following the corporation's waterlogging, the entire ten miles of Haweswater's circumference were left uninhabited save for the new Haweswater Hotel, partly built from the stones and slates of the submerged villages. The irony of this constructional cannibalism was that the salvaged antique materials ended up in high-end, state-of-the-art 1930s architectural fashion: Haweswater Hotel is an Art Deco confection, a stranded bankside setting for a Cluedo game.

When Wordsworth visited the Haweswater valley in the late nineteenth century for his *A Guide through the District of the Lakes*, he noted that it 'remains undefiled by the intrusion of bad taste', meaning tourism. It remains so. Haweswater is a wilderness, but one recreated by mankind. As I say, it is a place of paradox.

The disco-drizzled lights of the stone-faced hotel were our sole beacon in the ring of darkness, inn as lighthouse, and the pluvial night sky impenetrably overcast. After unpacking, I tentatively ventured out along the road in the rain alone, dog-less for once, and utterly torchless. I have never encountered such blackness, and it took actual concentration to discern the slight greyness of the lake and some staring into the primeval nothingness to figure the mountains opposite, these reduced to basic mass, characterless physics. So much for the majesty of the hills. Not the least character of the night is its distorting of perception and definition; water after dark is always more viscous-seeming than in daylight. Oily, even treacly. Or, at least this is true of flat bodies of water; the beck crashing down the hillside was a phosphorescent froth, a potion spewing from a devil's cauldron.

I was stumbling somewhere past the entrance to Old Corpse Road – so called because the bodies of the valley's dead were once carted over the hill to consecrated ground in Shap – when I noted a round white light hovering on the watery nothingness. Through the winter trees, as bare as driftwood, the light flickered. I am rarely, if ever, frightened by the night, but I was then.

It was the concatenation, of course: the impervious dark, the dog-lessness, the ominous cognomen of Old Corpse Road, the melancholia of Haweswater's submerged settlements, the wind manipulating the lakeside scrub . . . all combined to suggestibility. But for a nanosecond the floating globe defied my ability to explain it. I was plain-and-simply spooked. My consequent spine-shiver (the human equivalent of a fritted canine raising its hackles) was textbook, although the numbing of my upper legs may have been idiosyncratic.

The white sphere in the blackness was, it clicked, some sort of navigation aid, or warning light, but of definitely human provenance. I pressed ahead, not just because of the outbreak of rationality but because, surely, one of the purposes of nightwalking is the encouragement of self-reliance? The conquering of fear? As I neared the light I perceived it came from a tower – the water extraction facility for the Manchester Corporation's successor, United Utilities. I was not overly comforted on close approach: the tower is castellated, and would serve as an illustration for a Gothic novel: *The Tower of Haweswater*. I turned for the hotel, face-saving by blaming the rain. Later, in the drawing room, on a leather sofa beside the log fire and Jazz Age jazz piping on the music system, I had a glass of spirits to raise my spirits and banish the spiritual emanation I had imagined out on the dark water. The wind boomed startlingly in the chimney, and each of the thirty panes of the arched metal windows framed exact nocturnal black. The exorcism by alcohol was only partially successful. Which was glad tidings of a perverse sort. In that moment of fear before the spectral orb, I had learned a little humility, the mindset of the mouse. I had become too comfortable in darkness, always taking the well-travelled paths around home with canine company. When the night has lost all capacity for frisson and upsetting of the rational mind, it is diminished in its power.

Morning brought more rain. It was a day of a named storm, and the cresting, wind-whipped waves on the lake were omnidirectional and repetitive, like sea-tide. Benty Howe, the fell across the lake – this magnified in its width by the daylight, since diurnality enlarges view – was striped white by waterfalls.

Eventually, I tired of interiors; being inside too long always brings on a sort of self-loathing dolour. We drove to the south end of the lake, where the mountains curl around it akin to enormous sharp-spined dinosaurs slumbering under the grey rock and muted moorland grass. The signs of spring in the mountains were few; then again March itself is a month of paradox. The official first month of spring could equally be termed the last month of winter. Its Old English name was *Hlyda*, meaning 'loud', in recognition of its tendency to be stormy. Unruly. Hibernal. The only unambiguous primaveral portent was the budburst of the silver birch trees along the bank of the lake. From every twig small green flames erupted. Budburst. The darling budburst of March.

I'll say it myself. I scampered up Harter Fell like a mountain goat, or at least like the Lake District's local Herdwick sheep. Despite the rain, I enjoyed the musicality of the stoney Gatescarth path under my boots: the susurration on substrate, the decided bass *thonk* on slabs, the lovely *tink* of rolled pebbles. Sole music.

I should say 'scarpered up' Harter Fell, because I was a burglar scaling a ladder. It was a raid. No more. I needed to know the route for a night climb later. No one in their right mind scales an unknown mountain in the blindness of night.

There was no view from the top at 2,552 feet that afternoon: Harter Fell was cloud-capped, and the panoramic view denied to me. There was only the intimation of forbidding mountains all around, of being in Lakeland, England's own personal Himalayas. I wandered through the mist and thawing snow-sludge on the cairn-topped crown for a minute or two to confirm the route, before heading down.

Predictably, it was raining when I started my ascent of Harter Fell at night, and the chin of the new moon again failed to dint the cloud. The way up, though, was easy enough to discern through the black ink; the relative paleness of the stone path itself was an usher, as was its sonority under my boot. Besides, there was beside the path the Mardale beck, parallel and gushing, an auditory and visual handrail. The rain attacked my face in flint shards, and I squinted my way to the top.

It is, I tell you, quite a thing to stand alone on top of a mountain in winter in absolute surround darkness (the lowness of the cloud base suppressed the usual gleam of the northwestern conurbations). I was insig-nificant, a trivial atomic speck; I was magnificent, I was Adam, the first man and the last man of the universe. I was pathetic; I was powerful. I was awed supplicant before nature; I was roistering king, the world beneath my feet. I was suspended twixt earth and heaven.

The wind vortexed around me, and I feared to move my arms from my side in case I was spun upwards in my own personal ascension. (I was dressed in waterproofs, which tend to balloon alarmingly in the wind.) My head inadvertently started to play the hymn 'Nearer, My God, To Thee'. I tell you, the sheer exhilaration of it, I wanted to shout . . .

. . . Until I realized I could not breathe. The wind, supposedly the breath of life, was taking my breath away. I scurried from the summit; anyway, after such a figurative and metaphorical pinnacle of life the only way was down. The path seemed to spool endlessly down the U-shaped glacial gouge with its litter of boulders. For the umpteenth time in my life I pondered the paradox that descent, going with gravity, is harder work than ascent. I, the former nimble ovine of the afternoon, was reduced to alternating between plodding dobbin placing its hooves charily, or, to keep balance, the stooped Neanderthal from one of those 'The Progression of Man from Ape' illustrations in texts of palaeoanthropology.

Somewhere on the descent I became uneasy in my hypocrisy. I'd gone up Harter Fell wishing aloneness, for solitude on a night climb in the hills is an absolute given. But there came a point, stumbling down Gatescarth, when I craved familiarity. Something human.

Reaching the drystone wall which stretched up in a dim black line from the valley bottom was, then, a relief. Terra cognita. Built by shepherds long ago, the drystone walls of Cumbria, as with other upland areas of the nation where hedges fear to root, were constructed to divide rough grazing into manageable fields. The 150,000 miles of Britain's drystone walls are monuments of rurality, and indubitably Stone

Age. Drystone walling in these isles originates in the Neolithic period.

The shepherd-constructed drystone walls of Haweswater offered more than psychological solace that night. In the lee of a wall – a solved puzzle of precisely slotted Silurian slate – I took physical sanctuary, minutes of recuperation, and scoffed squares of Kendal mint cake. (A knowing homage, perhaps pretence; the Lakeland confection is favoured by real climbers, whereas I am an accidental hill walker.) Within arm's reach were splashes of pale lichen, vivid despite the dark and the rain. I once read that such drystone wall, as well as homing lichens and mosses, may support in excess of seventy-five vascular plants, making it a veritable 'rockery'.

On reaching the car park at the foot of the fell I thought I was done for the night, but the weather had an unexpected fit of clemency. The rain stopped and the wind dropped. The lake beckoned. I drove halfway back to the hotel, to where an overgrown United Utilities concrete ramp leads down to the water. If it was dark on the mountain, it was darker down here in this contender for the darkest place in England. I made slow progress down the moss-slicked ramp, as if learning to toddle, and walked slowly, arms in front of me for balance but also to discern obstacles in the way a fox's whiskers do. Only the lapping of the iron-odoured water indicated its edge, and to walk along the stoney lakeside I needed to feel with my hands, as well as carefully probe with my feet; there were boulders the shape and size of cars. It was absorbing nightwalking, a forced feeling for geology and its botany: the razor-edge of slate, water-smoothed pebbles (at one point I was on my hands and knees), the saw-toothed ferns in crevices, and once something so angular it must have man-made. I was reminded of my early efforts to learn the Braille of tree bark.

I lost track of time, but an oval rent suddenly appeared in the cloud, and through the lips of this hole stars fell on to the surface of the lake. There they illuminated the depths in columns, and I could see shoals of silver-scaled schelly, Haweswater's rare salmonid fish, a glacial relic, spinning and swarming through the doorways and windows of the ruined cottages of drowned Mardale Green and Measand. The English Atlantises.

A fantasia, of course. In daylight I stared at Haweswater's slate-grey surface and gained no depths of knowledge. But in those seconds of star-provoked imagination was there not some form of truth?

Night Notes: Nocturnality

Nocturnality: it obsesses me. The mystery of animal life out there in the darkness.

When the black curtain of night drops, the farmyard, the meadow, the hill, the river remain the same theatrical stage. But the cast changes. Where swallows lacily wheeled around the cow field in the sunshine comes the nightjar, hawking by hard angles in moonlight. Where butterflies fluttered in the after-noon garden, at midnight the pale ghosts of moths flicker around the honeysuckled arbour. In place of bees on the lane's verge, glow worms. Instead of the thrush chanting in the orchard, the nightingale ser-enading. At night, the desolate forest is no longer the hunting ground of the goshawk, but the long-eared owl.

With good reason almost 70 per cent of the world's animals are nocturnal. Animals that feed by night exploit sources of food that are also taken by day animals, but without coming into direct competition with them. Nature abhors waste, including wasted time. Nocturnality allows life around the clock. Also, daylight desiccates and is anathema to moist-skinned molluscs and amphibians. Above all, at night, it is easier to evade detection by predators. Darkness is concealment. It is at night that great mass migrations of British nature occur, the sweet coming of house martins, the dispersal of moles through the clover-perfumed grass, the eel migrations down the black, slithery river.

The night, of course, is not an entirely safe space. Out there in the dark prowl and patrol the nocturnal killers, with their special adaptations for hunting when the sun is gone from the world and humans are abed. The eye of the fox contains tapetum lucidum, a layer of reflective cells behind the retina, from the Latin for 'bright tapestry'; these cells reflect light back into the eye, so low-light vision is significantly enhanced. (The tapetum lucidum is the 'eyeshine' we see when we catch foxes in the car headlights on the lane.) Foxes also use their vibrissae, the sensory whiskers on their faces and legs; the fox's whiskers mean that it can 'feel' in the dark, finding its way between obsta-cles and along tunnels by detecting airflow. Nocturnal animals often have a nose for the job. A keen sense of smell in the blind night is an obvious advantage, as the twitchy wet-nosed snout of the hedgehog con-firms; it can detect a beetle's attar under three inches of soil.

The creatures of the night tend also to enjoy acute sensitivity to sound. Renard has hearing so keen – those permanently erect ears help – that it can remark a watch ticking at 60 feet. In absolute pitch-black night, tawny owls can discern shrews moving on the woodland floor by hearing alone, due to the owl's nerve-crammed asymmetric ears, which each receive sound at a slightly different volume and angle – and thus enable pinpoint killing.

Bats famously catch the moths, beetles and other insects that fly by night by transmitting high-frequency sound impulses and then interpreting the reflected echoes through their decidedly prominent ears. Echolocation. As early as 1793, Italian researcher Lazzaro Spallanzani demonstrated that, while blinded bats could find their way around their enclosure, deafened bats lost their sense of direction. So sophis-ticated is bat echolocation that these flying mammals, the world's only such, can detect a human hair in air.

Bat calls range from 9kHz to 200kHz. A human child may be able to hear their squeaks and clicks, the sound of internet dial-up. Most adults cannot, though I sometimes can detect noctules in ambient quiet. To produce the sound pulses of echolocation the bat's lar-ynx is conspicuously large, reinforced with bone, and the sound directed through a gap in the upper incisors. Horseshoe bats are an exception; the bat emits sound through its magnificent snozzle – which does indeed resemble a fleshy horseshoe – the folds of which tighten the focus of the sound beam. The nose job seems to bestow horseshoe bats with extra sensitivity, allowing them to locate insects at distances of 30 feet, whereas many bats only register insects at distances of circa 3.5 feet. Whatever, once any bat – and Britain has eighteen species – has sent out the call, the ear muscles relax and await the returning echo. Big ears help. The dumbo ears of the brown long-eared bat are quite nearly as long as its actual body. *Plecotus auritus* can detect a ladybird strolling over a leaf.

The long-eared bat, like others of its Chiroptera ilk, is locked in a millennia-old co-evolutionary arms race with its moth prey, with each species developing counter-measures to maintain survival. In an upping of their armoury, long-eared bats now use the sense of smell to help hunt moths. Meanwhile, choerocampine hawk-moths have evolved to hear with their mouthparts and respond to bat calls with evasive manoeuvres. Tiger moths (*Bertholdia trigona*) use their own ultrasound clicks to jam the echolocation signals of the big brown bat (*Eptesicus fuscus*). The world at night is a world at war.

The reason for the nocturnality of some animals is not always evident. The badger, for example, has no natural predators today. The presumption is that back in the primordial mist *Meles meles* feared gigantic foes, mega-fauna, that could only have been avoided by hiding down in the sett during the day.

Few nocturnal animals are active the whole night long, although the brown hare will put in a notably long shift – I've known a hare to eat for more than six hours of April darkness – since it is a creature with high calorific requirements; a hare needs 2,800kJ per day. Some animals will switch from being primarily diurnal in one season to principally nocturnal in another. Thus, in winter, salmonids, like the schelly of Haweswater, become principally nocturnal, hiding in refuges by day but emerging to feed at night. Some creatures only act out their roles at dusk and dawn. Properly, these latter are 'crepuscular'. Dusk and dawn are half-light, twilight, gloom. The animals that become active in the monochrome hours, the shadow time, such as rabbits, woodcock and red deer, exploit a distinct segment of the clock: there is just enough light to see, but it is dark enough to lower the odds of being caught and consumed. The bats that emerge earliest in the evening are usually fast-flying species, such as the noctule; they take to the greying sky at the moment the keen eyes of the diurnal sparrowhawk, kestrel, merlin, hobby, peregrine, harrier, eagle diminish in potency. The day sky is ridden by raptors. The tawny owl is determinedly nocturnal, thus more often heard than seen. There is sense to this: one study found that 73 per cent of tawny owls who died from natural causes were killed by diurnal birds of prey. Wisely, Old Brown refrains from hunting until the sparrowhawk with whom he shares the wood has gone to bed.

After dark, the sole British birds of prey a-wing are the owls and the moth-catcher that is the nightjar. And what birds they are. Assassins dressed in soft feathers. The nightjar, a summer migrant, scoops up, swift-like, its aerial insect prey, the staple being moths, but a favourite morsel being the dor beetle (*Geotrupes stercorarius*), the black beetle that flies after sunset. Hence the nightjar's old name of dor hawk, familiar in East Anglia and on Exmoor. The sky at night, though, belongs truly to the owl. The retina of the owl contains few cones and abundant rods, meaning they are, in plain speak, sublime at spotting prey in extremely low light. The eyes of a long-eared owl almost fill its skull and the bird can detect a mouse in a football stadium lit by a single candle.

The owl, the plumed lord of the dark, brings death on noiseless wings. Owls have comb-like serrations on the leading edge of the wings and a velvety fringe on the trailing edge to dampen noise. The British owls are a cunningly feathered lot, camouflaged to pass as tree pieces for their daytime lying-in, mere faint cloud shapes in the sky at night. The barn owl, with its blaring white belly, is no exception. Any rat chancing to look up sees in that chest the full moon moving across the heavens.

Out a-hunting at night, the hunter animal is soft-winged, soft-padded, yet night in the countryside is far from noiseless. In lonely hours, in wood and field and on riverbank, the silence is ripped apart by the screams of rats as the talons of the owl grip their backs and the wail of rabbits as the trap-jaw of the badger closes. There are cries of life, as well as death, for how else does one advertise for a blind date in the blind dark if not by crying out loud? The eeriest sound of a winter night in Britain, creepier than the wind moaning around the gables, is the mating call of the fox, a reminder itself that the music of night varies by season.

Summer nights are made musical by nightingales in trees and grasshoppers chirping from the meadow grass, serenaders both. If singing or 'stridulating' (to give the grasshopper's sound, caused by limb-friction, its scientific label) such love songs is not an option, there is always a perfumed invitation card. Otter females deposit scent marks in their urine, advertising their reproductive status, around the riverbank. Noisome, as opposed to noisy. The female glow worm (*Lamprohiza splendidula*) lights up the night to attract a flying mate. Luciferin, secreted by the insect's glands, is broken down by oxygen in the presence of the enzyme luciferase. And lo! There is glow. Three bars on the abdomen illuminate; the light is piercing, like the dot you get if you refract sunshine through a magnifying glass.

To see a group of glow worms is to see stars on Earth.

So small, though, the human audience to watch the miracle plays of night-time nature.

Week-night Service

The five old bells
Are hurrying and eagerly calling,
Imploring, protesting
They know, but clamorously falling
Into gabbling incoherence, never resting
Like spattering showers from a bursten sky-rocket
    dropping
In splashes of sound, endlessly, never stopping.

The silver moon
That somebody has spun so high
To settle the question, yes or no, has caught
In the net of the night's balloon,
And sits with a smooth bland smile up there in the sky
Smiling at naught,
Unless the winking star that keeps her company
Makes little jests at the bells' insanity,
As if he knew aught!

The patient Night
Sits indifferent, hugged in her rags,
She neither knows nor cares
Why the old church sobs and brags;

The light distresses her eyes, and tears
Her old blue cloak, as she crouches and covers her face,
Smiling, perhaps, if we knew it, at the bells' loud
    clattering disgrace.

The wise old trees
Drop their leaves with a faint, sharp hiss of contempt,
While a car at the end of the street goes by with a laugh;
As by degrees
The poor bells cease, and the Night is exempt,
And the stars can chaff
The ironic moon at their ease, while the dim old church
Is peopled with shadows and sounds and ghosts that lurch
In its cenotaph.

D. H. Lawrence

Part III

Around the Barley Field and into the Summer Wood

I T WAS NEARING midnight, and there was no real need to see the barley again. The combine harvester was coming the next morning, the date set in digital, as unrelenting as stone, as definite as Moses' tablet. The grains of the sun-goldened barley heads had been run through several hands, and when squeezed found to be firm but milky inside, which in lay language meant 'ripe for harvest'. But moonlight was lying on the lane, as open as an invitation. A country lane exists, waits, to progress you practically from A to B. When illuminated by a summer moon a lane will also actively entice. Be a beckoning. This is doubly true when the verges are lined with the flowerheads of white campion lumining as bright as streetlamps. *Silene latifolia*, unlike most wild-flowers, remains open after dusk and develops more of an aroma at night. If I sniffed hard enough I could just detect the scent, an intense floral honey, which is catnip to moths, its primary pollinators. Night-flying moths, of which Britain has over 2,000 types, are wholly unappreciated. They are more efficient pollinators than bees.

Even at night something of the slender, metre-high elegance of white campion – the 'Silene' of the scientific comes from the Greek forest god, Silenus – was evident. Indeed, nocturnality is white campion's friend, not just for the pollinating activities of moths: darkness hides the ugly aspects of the flower, the fat 'bladders' (calyx) which lurk behind the radiant blooms. And the hairy stems.

The air was heated and heavy with the scent of wild honeysuckle in the hedge and of the new hay in the barn. Ghost moths, *Hepialus humuli*, danced a nocturnal slow sarabande. If I had closed my eyes I would have declared myself inside an oriental garden.

With the usual Labrador, I started up the hill; the angle of the moonlight was such that, when I looked back, the canine and I formed one gigantic, articulated six-legged being, a shadow beast escaped from an illustrated book on fabulous animals. Or ancient mythology. The rasping of the crickets, my bootsteps on chalk gravel, the breath of dog – these were the night's cadence. Halfway up the hill, we saw a black fox running, as smooth as a silk streamer over the blanched hayfield. The Labrador, tensed, factored vectors, distance, speed, and settled for preservation of dignity disguised as protective love of her owner, and remained at heel. Up to that point the scent of the evening was sweet; but some sly waft carried our stink to the fox, which arrested, saw us. Screamed. It was a savage cry, an aurality from another time: Before Man. As if cued to persist the theme as we entered a tree-tunnel narrowing, an owl in an oak hissed. One expects owls to be folksy, funny, familiar Shakespearian *tu-whit*ters, fluffy toys for cooey babies. This owl emitted a snake-sound, resentful of our trespass upon her secret arbour. A shiver of wind repeatedly inflated the oak, deflated it, in a rapid nervous breathing.

The dog and I drew closer but pressed on to the top of the hill, to emerge in the broad, warm moonlight upland, and there was the barley field, spilling on to the verge like cresting surf. We took the rutted track alongside the wood, so the full expanse of the barley sea with its frame of trees could be seen. A hare sat on the track, washing its paws puss-like in the moon's argentine plating. A charm for a necklace.

We stood, dog and I, before the acres of barley, and marvelled as the warm breeze-blown moonshine flowed creamily through the crop, which sometimes swayed, other times spoon-stirred. Once, after an anticipatory shimmy, the whole five acres stood motionless, then parted in the middle, as though run through by a comb held by an invisible hand. It was unnerving; it was fascinating too. The barley that night-danced to many tunes, performed choreographies known only to Demeter. (Poor wheat, with its heavy head, managed only a jiggle next door.) Even the slightest hint of a zephyr would encourage the delicate blond barley heads with their fine hair to s-w-i-n-g, and in so doing make their own musical crescendo, s-w-i-s-h, which may be likened to the sound of jazz drum brushes on brass.

Is there not art in such a scene? If it were transferred to Tate Modern as a living, kinetic installation, 'The Barley Ballet', would it not be hailed? Acclaimed if placed, miniaturized, on top of the Fourth Plinth in Trafalgar Square? Do we not overlook how farming beautifies landscape? Or at least a certain sort of agriculture. The barley field on the top of the hill is low-chemical 'regenerative', and the wild flora played their part in the moon dance. With closed-up heads the black poppies circled in a slow, lost trance, the skeletons of the wild oats quivered, a ghostly theatrical shaking; the thistles twisted, minimalistically; the field bindweed clasped its partner, the barley itself. During the last weeks the green bine of *Convolvulus arvensis* had climbed up the stout barley stalks and its flowers trumpeted its success.

Such a field has its behind-the-curtain secrets, as well as its staged performance. The dog and I were next to a 'smeuse', a hole in the side of the barley, the open mouth of a hidden passage running deep into the crop made by an animal, perhaps the charming hare. Many years ago, the author Kit Williams buried a jewelled gold hare, sparking off a national treasure hunt for his 'Masquerade'.

It has always seemed to me, however, that a golden barley field, where real hares hide, has properly priceless mysteries. By the time of tonight's Barley Ballet I had watched the field for five months, from its spring sowing until that eve of harvest. The crop had succoured many things, from skylarks to field mice, from red-legged partridge to orange-tip butterflies. Swallows had cheered it on with their chatter, and the sun had rescued it from the recrudescence of flood with salvationist rays.

I thought I knew the barley, but on the night of the Barley Ballet I saw, high up on especially tall and stout fennel in the crop, a weasel. The little predator was clasping the main stem of the plant while standing on one of its flat flower heads, much as a human lookout might stand on the spar and clasp the mast of a schooner at sea. I suppose that the weasel, the first I had seen in an age, was surveilling the scene, planning the hunt.

But it looked as if it too was enjoying the last dance of the barley.

Under the full fat moon, I returned home via the Ten Acre Wood, because one can become greedy for wonders, and I knew the nightjars would be about. Sure enough, as we entered the tunnel entrance to the wood, I heard their transmissions; they do not sing, as other birds do, but 'churr'; an unnatural, manufactured, repetitive tool-type sound, as suggested by the archaic common names for this summer migrant bird: 'scissor grinder', 'razor grinder', 'spinner'. The male nightjar has evolved to call continuously, altering amplitude and pitch to inhale as it emits 1,900 notes a minute.

My ears attuned, I discerned three nightjars calling, although the sound seemed to surround me on four sides. This was not purely my imagining. Nightjars are ventriloquists, the males swivelling their head as they purr, so their song pours down their backs, and swirls around upon itself. Ventriloquism in birdsong is defence, the purpose to deceive predators as to the location of the singer who is perched in the open (although the bird's vermiculated greys, browns, blacks make it a sublime physical mimicry of the tree bough it rests upon). Since nightjars hunt visually, they need some luminescence in the sky, against which their insect prey can be silhouetted; thus, twilight or moonlight, like tonight. The mouth of the nightjar is wide, gaping, openable on two planes, vertical and horizontal, fringed by bill bristles which funnel cruelly the prey into the mouth-trap. A moth-trap.

The chalk-stone track of the wood is tractor-wide, and arrow-straight for 500 yards through telephone-pole oaks. No bends, an open aspect, free absolutely from the inconvenient obstacles called branches if you are a hunting night bird. In moonshine, the wood

track is a moth run, a moth shoot; a nightjar's perfect killing ground. From the trees, moths emerged, white and hapless, pathetically fluttery. A nightjar came whirling in over our heads, performing its own ballet. A danse macabre. A pirouette on the centre of its own spine, then a leap, a swoop, a dead-stop, every wing and tail feather air-braking.

The bird's agility extends to the courtship display, where it flies whirlwind circles while clapping its wings together over its back. There's a place in the wood where the woodsman came and razed the trees save for five Scots pine: a forest glade, a natural theatre in the round, a rural Globe Theatre. The nightjars love it – the sound of a chainsaw cutting into a tree is not always the scream of sacrilege – and I went there, plonked myself down at the base of a pine, the dog beside me. No nightjars came; a human arrogance, of course, to expect nature to perform to our desires. In the night-time wood I slapped at mosquitoes, fidgeted because of the crested bark behind my shirt. It was a moment when I remembered why I am word-perfect on the library scene in Oscar Wilde's *The Decay of Lying*, with Vivian's lament:

> *Enjoy Nature! I am glad to say that I have entirely lost that faculty . . . Nature is so uncomfortable. Grass is hard and lumpy and damp, and full of dreadful black*

insects. Why, even [William] Morris's poorest workman could make you a more comfortable seat than the whole of Nature can.

Anyone who tells you nature is endlessly lovely is someone who endlessly fails to go out into nature.

Why did I stay, sitting there for an hour or more late at night? Prosaically, lethargy; it seemed as hard to get up as sit put. There felt too a duty to record such a marvellous night, which I duly did in the notebook I always have on me. Verbatim:

Animals/birds seen/heard at 11.05–11.55 p.m.

Tawny owl, occasional contact call.
Robin (a surprisingly consistent night singer, taking the limelight).
Nightjar (reprise).
Shrews, constant crepitation. [Another animal, like bats, that uses echolocation.]
Crickets ditto.
Fox (1 alarm bark).
Moths, from brambly bush, issuing.

Squealing of a rabbit, death-gripped by an owl or fox
    or badger.
Keening of the small warm-blooded things amid
    trees, perpetual.
(Labrador snoring.)
The vacuous yapping of a farm dog in the distance,
    irritating the night, although producing a wry smile.
Hedgehog, with its smoker's snuffle.
Long-eared bats, making mazy cut-out shadows
    which fall on the woodland floor.
Stag beetles riding the air, Harley Davidson-style.
Smells: gorse, which is cloves and Bible fables;
    the resinous shower gel of the pine; and at the
    periphery of discern, borne on warm wafting,
    honeysuckle, floral Chanel.

And then the *post scriptum*: behind me, hidden by the bole of the pine, a bestial *grrr*-ing, alarming to the uninitiated, wryly amusing to the woodland maven: a roe deer buck calling for a mate. A rude and antique sound in the British landscape; archaeological evidence of roe in these isles dates to the Mesolithic period, 10,000 to 6000 BC. The nativeness of the roe has caused distinct evolutionary traits, notably the earliness of the rutting season (the other five species of deer running wild in the UK mate in autumn).

The roe buck moved off, to continue his amorous nocturnal rambling, but stopped, adolescent-angry, testosteroned-up, to butt a hazel bush with his antlers. (All of this was heard, never viewed.) Roe bucks are strongly territorial, their fiefdom primarily woodland and woodland edge, which they mark by scent, including from the horns, and urine. One feels for does, given that deer possess 250 million olfactory receptors, compared to our five million.

The above notes, the bare bones, require some adumbration. Few birds sing by night, but more will call. But whether song or call, the sound of the birds in woodland is seasonal. In this same place in June a cuckoo called at 10.32 p.m., its two-note bassoon boom an occlusion of robin's wistful contemplation. Bird sound is an allotment of ephemera.

There were perhaps ten long-eared bats hunting on their fluttery, long, leather wings, and at one stage they settled into a circular, anti-clockwise rotation, a bat-pack waltz. By accident or design, this corralled a shoal of moon-backed moths into the centre of the glade, where they made easy pickings.

The flight of the bats, which descended to head height of a sitting man, seemed to stir the scents of the glade and the warm, lustral earth into a potpourri I wanted to bottle and take home. Then that nebulous thing, the quality of moonlight in the summer wood. Less precise than the moonlight of winter; more diffuse, softer. More ethereal. Beneath my tree, I was in the front row of the theatre where nature ruled.

As the dog, roused from her slumber, and I exited the doors of the wood from deep within the trees came the bone-thump of roe deer antlers being locked.

An August Midnight

I

A shaded lamp and a waving blind,
And the beat of a clock from a distant floor:
On this scene enter – winged, horned, and spined –
A longlegs, a moth, and a dumbledore;
While 'mid my page there idly stands
A sleepy fly, that rubs its hands . . .

II

Thus meet we five, in this still place,
At this point of time, at this point in space.
– My guests besmear my new-penned line,
Or bang at the lamp and fall supine.
'God's humblest, they!' I muse. Yet why?
They know Earth-secrets that know not I.

Thomas Hardy

Night Notes: An Ode to a Nightingale (and a Woodlark)

Do nightingales still sing in Berkeley Square? Do nightingales sing anywhere much, any more?

It's the saddest song I have ever heard, the song of the nightingale bird. Sadder now that the nightingale's nocturnes, once familiar, seem like requiems for its own extinction and its habitat, too, which is that of unofficial, thickety countryside or traditionally coppiced woodland. And pure night.

The Ancients early noted the musical melancholia of this nondescript avian, this beige bird. Homer in *The Odyssey* scribed, on some stone tablet, of the 'wailing' of the nightingale in the groves, but Ovid overdid it, making the nightingale's song a tortured tale of rape and revenge. In *Metamorphoses*, Philomela is raped by Tereus and, at the moment of her revenge, both protagonists are turned by the gods into birds: Philomela into a nightingale.

For a millennium and more, from the Romans to the Romantics, the nightingale was exclusively Philomela of melancholic mood. Some, as the Bard of Avon did, gave Philomela's torment a prurient quiver. Thus, in *The Rape of Lucrece*, Shakespeare has: 'Come,

Philomel[a]; that sing'st of ravishment / [. . .] And whiles against a thorn thou bear'st thy part, / To keep thy sharp woes waking.'

The poetic cult of Philomela reached its pitch, of course, in 'Ode to a Nightingale' by John Keats, the Romantics' Romantic, published over two hundred years ago. Inspired by a nightingale singing at his Hampstead home (not that far, as the nightingale flies, from Berkeley Square), he found in Philomela's grief the exact consuming story of his own unhappiness: he had been diagnosed with tuberculosis.

Sometimes, at night, I, too, find dolefulness in your tones, Nightingale, such as when I am alone in the house (my version of your bowl-like nest of herbage), my wife away visiting her aunt, fledglings flown. But night is night, darkness, the time of the Death Watch, the riding of witches, the incoming tide of blackest memory.

Even the scientists, with their dry-as-dust classification of you, Nightingale, into the oscine suborder of the passerine order, accepted the sorrow arising from your syrinx as being defining; your scientific tag is *Luscinia megarhynchos*, from *luctus*, meaning lamentation.

Did you know?

Poor Nightingale, there is so much more to you than the purveyor of sad songs, the prop of mopey poets and the patron bird-saint of the sleepless. Instead of the all-encompassing glooming, might we not consider instead the beauty in your voice, an aesthetic ideal to which our human music can only aspire? Because Keats got this right: you have 'full-throated ease' when singing.

I've been to national opera, I possess the Deutsche Grammophon CD of the Vienna Philharmonic conducted by Böhm performing Mozart's Piano Concerto No. 27, I've listened to Gregorian chants in Gothic cathedrals – but the greatest musical performance I ever heard was outside my bedroom one night this spring.

It was mild and it was dry (how nightingales like it), my family was home (how I like it), the windows were open and there streamed in nothing but starlight and the singing of five nightingales from the scrubby walnut orchard.

They sang the old favourite hymns, passed down the years from nightingale to nightingale, and I, in my turn, remembered Izaak Walton's note to self that the man who hears at midnight the singing of the nightingale 'might well be lifted above earth, and say, Lord, what Musick hast thou provided for the Saints in Heaven, when thou affordest bad men such musick on earth?'

It was joyous, that divine performance at a stone house in a quiet corner of rambly, brambly countryside, and if I had to describe what you sounded like I would write: 'Like spring water rising from the rocks of a South Down at sheepy twilight.' The Victorians would never have caged you for entertainment, Nightingale, if minor key was all you had.

Quite apart from your defiant gurgling happiness, your performance that night would have perplexed poor Keats even more on discovering your gender: contrary to the tradition of Philomela, only unpaired male nightingales sing regularly at night. Neither do you like to be, contra the cult of Philomela once again, a soloist. Your preference is to be in a loose, spread-out fugue outfit, riffing off your fellows.

Oh, much mythed bird. Nightingale, you sing by day, as well as by night. Only in poesy are you matutinally mute. Yes, you are secretive and shy, except if singing, when no real caution at all is required to get up close to you. My wife and I walk a back lane with the dogs; you perch on a hazel arch singing away and bat not a lid over your delicate eyes as we pass under. (Those lovely brown eyes, I suppose, are the one corporeal clue, with the glorious chestnut of the tail plumes, of the exotic music that lies within your modest being.) Rarely, Nightingale, do you sing at any great height, another reason why you appeal to us humans so. You are within reach. Almost. You're not a sky-god like the swift, or a skulky, marginal moorland creature like the snipe. From your straggling struggle here in April from Africa, you'll sing for a month or so, but I've heard you, yearning for a mate, as late as the second week of July. (I suppose, with your numbers declined by 90 per cent in five decades – my lifetime – a mate is ever harder to find.) Yes, I heard your desperate yearning. You see, no one is wrong to find sadness in the nightingale's song – or, indeed, joy, yearning or other emotions – because who today can say for certain that birds are without feelings, plural and various? Almost every day, scientists discover that some animal has 'emotional intelligence'. Today, it's cows; yesterday, it was sheep. Tomorrow, it will be birds. They will have their day.

If any bird can express emotions, it is you, Nightingale, with your breviary of 260 songs, all using trills and tweets, whistles and *jug-jugs*, rattles and rasps, chirps and flutings, both ascending and descending in pitch. John Clare, the naturalist's Romantic poet, wished to add to your recorded repertoire, rightly:

> '*Wew-wew wew-wew chur-chur chur-chur*
> *Woo-it woo-it*' – *could this be her*
> '*Tee-rew tee-rew tee-rew tee-rew*
> *Chew-rit chew-rit*' – *and ever new*

Perhaps, Nightingale, you pluck our soul-strings because, inside that small brown body, you have, in some miniature and crude form, similar chords of feeling. Or, perhaps, when we were primitive and lived in trees, when the world was new, we sang like you – we share fifty genes or more to do with sound-making. Perhaps, when you sing in our quiet corners, we hear the echo of our singing selves two million years ago, before we fashioned speech, made words. Fancy! We may have once sung like the birds. Like you even, Nightingale.

But you have competition, Nightingale, for the

laurels as lead nocturnal chorister! Did you know? For the little woodlark, *Lullula arborea*, will also put on a show under the stars, trilling its spring song from any prominent perpendicular perch, from gatepost to telephone post, though preferring a tree. Well, the clue is in the Latin tag, you see. The song of the woodlark is . . . something like cousin skylark's but less spirited, more reflective, and interjected with a distinct liquid *lu-lu-lu* sound. The bird really does do what it says on its label. Gerard Manley Hopkins tried gamely, and not without worth, to transliterate the bird's song into mere human words:

> Teevo cheevo cheevio chee:
> *O where, what can that be?*
> Weedio-weedio: *there again!*
> *So tiny a trickle of song-strain*
> *And all round not to be found*
> *For brier, bough, furrow, or green ground*
> *Before or behind or far or at hand*
> *Either left either right*
> *Anywhere in the sunlight.*
> *Well, after all! Ah but hark –*
> '*I am the little woodlark.*
> *[. . .]*
> *Through the velvety wind V-winged*

To the nest's nook I balance and buoy
With a sweet joy of a sweet joy,
Sweet, of a sweet, of a sweet joy
Of a sweet – a sweet – sweet – joy.'

The woodlark's song is fragile and fleeting, always behind the next turn in the path and 'not to be found'.

The French composer Olivier Messiaen includes you, Woodlark, in his *Catalogue d'oiseaux* (1956–8), where you briefly sing with another bird. Complementary and contrapuntal. Neither outshines the other. The duet of the woodlark and nightingale.

To the Nightingale

Oh Nightingale that on yon bloomy spray
Warblest at eve, when all the woods are still;
Thou with fresh hope the lover's heart dost fill,
While the jolly hours lead on propitious May.
Thy liquid notes that close the eye of day,
First heard before the shallow cuckoo's bill,
Portend success in love; O, if Jove's will
Have linked that amorous power to thy soft lay,
Now timely sing, ere the rude bird of hate
Foretell my hopeless doom in some grove nigh:
As thou from year to year hast sung too late
For my relief, yet hadst no reason why:
Whether the Muse, or Love, call thee his mate,
Both them I serve, and of their train am I.

John Milton

Part IV

Tideline

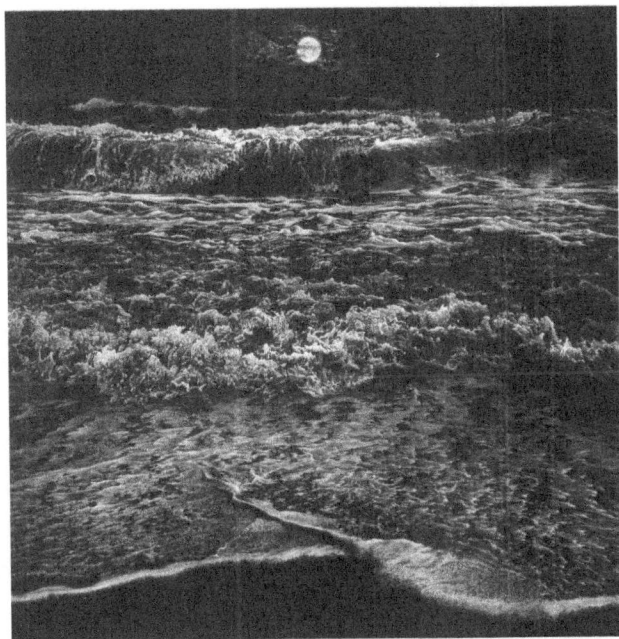

STRUGGLING OVER THE heavy shingle we came to the rock pools under the black cliff, picking our way by the feeble light of the wetted seafront street-lamps. There was a black cloak of cloud over our heads. In one weed-fringed pool, a dead herring gull floated like a funereal white water lily. Two living gulls, borne by the harsh wind off the water, drifted silently over-head, the deceased bird's guardian spirits I assumed. Or perhaps the disembodied souls of dead sailors. There was no music to the sea, unless you count cacophony. The white waves crashed and grasped jealously at the beach, dragging stones into the depths. Behind the breaking waves and the sea defences the tar-dark Irish Sea was formless.

There is an ineffable melancholy to a small Welsh seaside town on a cold winter's night, and Borth on Cardigan Bay is not an exception; the cafe-cum-gift-shop shut, the queue at the chip shop sufficiently small for the door to be closed, and only one smoker outside the Victoria Inn on the long-running High Street, which is the one street. The wind plucked the metal stays on the beached boats beside the lifeboat station, so they pinged monotonously against the masts.

Borth in January. A time and place to make your own entertainment. Earlier, in the afternoon, my daughter, an adherent of wild swimming no matter the weather or season, had 'gone for a dip', and this without a wetsuit. (The gaggle of surfers, sealy-skinned in rubber, were nonplussed.) The thermal shock would have killed me, and I assigned myself the job of event photographer. What to do at night, though? Rock-pooling with a £10 ultraviolet torch was one answer. Or, at least it was for us. Out on the rocks we were alone.

A rock pool is the cruellest of habitats for nature; doused in saline solution twice a day, and left desiccated by the retreating tide twice a day. And yet temperate in its way, since the coastal zone in Britain rarely freezes, and calm when the last finger of tide has withdrawn. A rock pool is a natural aquarium with a surfeit of strange marine things which glow stranger still at night under UV light. By day the body of a snakelocks anemone is brown; in UV shine it lumined alien neon green, which was also the hue of choice of common shrimps. Beige seashells lit up in high-vis orange, and seaweeds, diurnally drab, turned garishly mauve in UV. Green shore crabs became blue shore crabs, and a sea spider fluoresced in Halloween green. Why do these sea creatures glow? It's a form of communication for some species; for others it is a warning to would-be predators. Many intertidal species are more active at night; the rocks ran with hermit crabs, finny blennies swam in plain sight. A rock pool that by day seemed a deserted backwater, by night Piccadilly-bustled. In a quiet alcove of the black cliff we stood cock-eared, listened to scores of limpets feeding, their toothy-tonguey radulas rasping seaweed spores off the rocks. Even above the sound of the surf the crackle of the shellfish devouring could be heard.

The rock pool illuminations a true seaside entertainment. But odd. Had the plethora of rock pools been cameos of miniature futuristic cities they could not have been more fantastical.

The tide was coming in, and we still wanted things to do. Nightwalking along the shore was the mermaid's call. Besides, the clouds were being driven back, and stars appearing over the sea, another siren invite. We debated under the lamp next to the RNLI ramp, the lamp-shine falling on upturned seashells falsely pearlescent, artificially nacreous. In we end we decided to nightwalk at the far end of town where the sand dunes of Ynyslas village border both the sea and the Dovey Estuary. We drove there; the distance is over two miles. Borth has the longest beach in Ceredigion.

As we swung on to the estuary sand to park, the car headlamps caught a rabbit in their glare. We assign species to habitats. Nature is not so easily pigeon-holed. The flat grass beds amid the dunes abound with rabbits, as one expects. A nocturnal rabbit out on the sand chomping samphire is unforeseen. Except perhaps by the Leporidae themselves.

Ours was the only car, and there was no one to collect the £4 parking charge. Across the black blankness of the estuary the seafront of Aberdovey, Borth's more genteel Georgian cousin.

The Ynyslas dunes, part of the Dyfi National Nature Reserve, are a family favourite. We took the known path from the estuary to the sea, 520 metres through the looming mountains of the moon, the roaring sea beyond an aural compass. Venus revealed itself in the west, a guiding light. The dunes are a wild place even in daylight, and, unlike the town, are defenceless against the sea. The air was thick and saline, and the marram grass on the dunes bristled and whistled. A repeated thought as I proceeded cautiously, torchless: who made this sandy path? The parallel path to the south is a tourist boardwalk. But our path, narrow and twisting, up mound, down mound, was of other, older origin; in places it was pounded trench-deep, light-less chasms on the dark side of the moon. While some human footpaths follow animal tracks, rabbits are not great waymakers. Fishermen, perhaps, taking a shortcut from samphire- and cockle-gathering on the estuary to casting long lines into the sea. The marine economy of Borth was always intimate and inshore, its business lobster pots and laverbread, its inhabitants dwelling in low stone cottages painted in pastel blues and pinks. A bounden intimacy between shore and sea.

There were times on the path when I groped my way, the tips of marram grass sharp on my fingers. Confidence aided progression; I had a lifetime map of the route in my head. The smoothness of the handrail on the short wooden walkway was familiar.

Hubris. On an incline I stalled, suddenly aware that solidity to my right had disappeared. 'Not that way, keep left,' said my daughter behind me. On these dunes where she had once stumbled and sprawled as a toddler, she had aided me. I turned on the torch for the first time; we were beside a 30-foot drop down the sandy side of a dune, a lacuna in space and mind.

On we went, trepidatious in our tread, until we emerged on the high shingle bank of the shore, and scuffled down it to the beach, where the flat sand was studded by rocks. By now there were stars galore over the sea, and over the sea the stars have special value. Once upon a time, before the compass, all sailors had to navigate at night over the watery waste were the stars and the planets.

We went north along the beach, towards the distant bead of bright lights of Aberdovey promenade, our progress slowed by the rocks, which became more foot-catchingly irregular. I wanted to resist the torch because its On button always dims the senses. A wiser head prevailed: 'We won't do much walking with broken ankles.' Switching on the torch we tacked to higher ground, softer sand, crossing a bed of lifeless clam shells which splintered sacrilegiously under our feet, as rude as breaking bone china; the torch beam illuminated a sandcastle of Plateresque extravagance, with a tower decorated by cockle shells and a wall of refulgent quartz. I was put in mind instantaneously of our family summer holidays here in this spot an eon ago; the sun-haze, the jovial jumping waves, horses and cars modelled from sand (one for a girl, one for a boy) and the search for dry sticks for a campfire. And the August night when my ears delighted in the wailing of a raft of Manx shearwaters offshore; the summer visiting seabird only enters its burrow home after dark, hence 'night bird'.

On the band between dunes and shells we sailed ahead torchless, navigating through fabulous driftwood creatures – a giant dachshund, a gargantuan albino worm, the antlers of a buried Ice Age elk – until we rounded the headland on to the strand of the estuary. It was an emergence into tranquillity, like entering an immense darkened cathedral. The windswept dunes are also a windbreak. There were now more sounds than the hissing selfish sea; there was the piping of oyster catchers, an always restless bird; something put up a small flock of waders, which squeaked their displeasure in an ever-diminishing circle around our heads; and a solitary curlew cried its own name into the vast estuarine emptiness. A sort of haunting:

> *Of the moon, as it slowly mounts the skies.*
> *Then from the mere come plaintive cries!*
>
> *Is it the shriek of a spectre dread,*
> *Wraith of a murdered man long dead?*
> *No! 'Tis not from a phantom throng;*
> *'Tis only the lonely curlews' song.*

R. M. Ingersley,
'The Night Song of the Curlew', *c.* 1911

Of the birds of the estuary environment, the curlew is the truest night-liver. It feeds by feel, not by sight, its sensitive bill-tip able to detect prey in the ooze. (Female curlews have longer bills than males so they do not compete for food.) A certain disconcerting human quality exists in the curlew's call, hence the folkloric association with the dead, the spiritual and the sinister. In Scotland and the North of England the bird is the 'whaup', sharing the cognomen with a goblin reputed to go around houses after nightfall with a long beak resembling a pair of tongs with which it carries off evil-doers. Curlews flying overhead presage death.

It was a U-shaped voyage. After some forty minutes we were heading back to the car. We had to be. The dunes were to our right, Aberdovey twinkled on the black water behind us, and the sensible emptiness of the Dyfi estuary to our left; the Dyfi comes out of the mountainous heart of Wild Wales. Above us were the stars, the original navigation aid for night wanderers as well as sailors. Sirius fixed the course over the sands, which shifted between deeply soft and deeply wet. Whichever way we trod, however, came a sinking feeling until we discovered the tideline of deposited seaweed, wind-dried and mat-like. Further up the estuary, a curlew cried, then another.

The longer one walks in the blind dark, the quicker and keener the senses. 'That's water!' we both said in the same instant. The estuary had sidled up beside us, quiet and esurient. Our path reduced to being between a quag and a soft place. It started raining.

Then I heard the *ank ank* of geese; the Dyfi estuary is the winter abode of both barnacle geese and Greenland white-fronted geese. I do not know which breed flew above us, but like us they were star sailors. I do know that their baying filled the cavernous dark until my ears rang, and the threshing of their invisible wings was as wind which almost lifted us off our feet and carried us to the car.

'The man who invented electric seats,' said my daughter, 'was a genius.'

Night Notes: Under the Plough Moon

*Mortal as I am, I know that I am born for
a day. But when I follow at my pleasure the
serried multitude of the stars in their circular
course, my feet no longer touch the earth.*

Ptolemy (flourished AD 127–145 in
Alexandria, Egypt)

I like the old ways of farming, sometimes the very
old ways, with their rituals and experience-wrought
calendars. Last night, 9 November, I went out of the
back door to check the stars: the Plough was there,
because it is always there, almost risibly bright in its
dominance and expanse in the northern sky. I held my
left arm up in a crooked-arm salute; and the Plough,
standing on its handle, surpassed it in extent.

The Plough is not a constellation, as every astron-
omer under the moon will wish to tell you, but an
asterism, a number of stars which make a recognizable
shape. Astronomically, the seven stars of the Plough
form part of the body of Ursa Major, the Great Bear
constellation. In Ancient Greek *arktos* is 'bear' and
hence we term the far north of our planet the Arctic

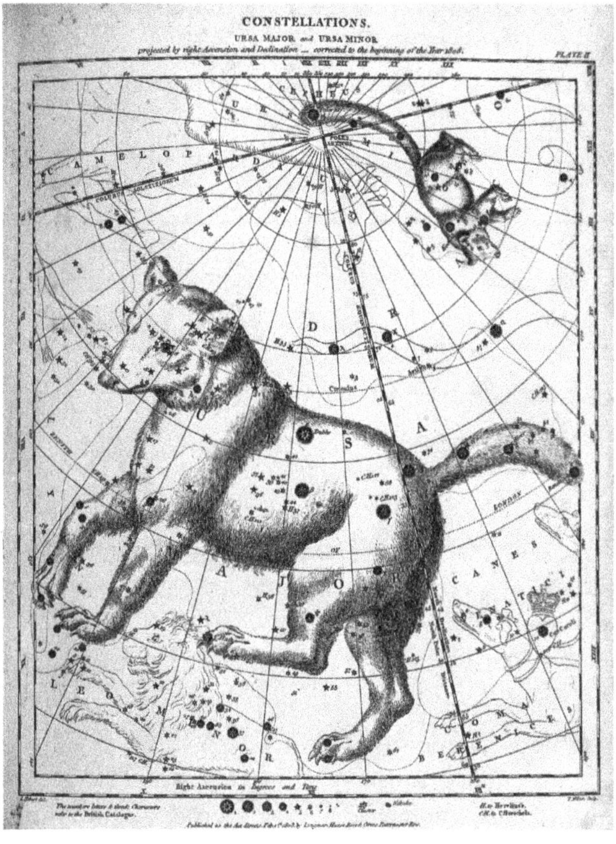
CONSTELLATIONS.
URSA MAJOR and URSA MINOR
projected by right Ascension and Declination ... corrected to the beginning of the Year 1808.
PLATE II
D
R
A
C
O
U
R
S
A
M
J
CANES
VENATICI
L
E
O
M
I
N
O
R
COMA BERENICES
Right Ascension in Degrees and Time
The numbers letters & Greek Characters refer to the British Catalogue.
H. to Hevelius.
C.H. to C. Herschels.

since its lies under the Great Bear. And it was Arctic-cold last night.

The small sorority that are the Pleiades, primarily winter stars, had become visible in recent days. These stellar daughters of Atlas featured prominently as prompts in the ancient agricultural almanacs. Hesiod, the Greek poet who flourished around 700 BC, remarked in his poem, the *Works and Days*:

> *And if longing seizes you for sailing the stormy seas,*
> *when the Pleiades flee mighty Orion*
> *and plunge into the misty deep*
> *and all the gusty winds are raging,*
> *then do not keep your ship on the wine-dark sea*
> *but, as I bid you, remember to work the land.*

The Pleiades start fleeing Orion and setting just before dawn ('plunge into the misty deep') during October.

To our superstitious ancestors the movements and configuration of the stars and planets were portentous events. Or maybe our ancestors, agriculturalists almost all, were simply sensible. October going on November is the time to commence working your plot, meaning to plough and to sow. Before the advent of clocks the progress of the planets informed farmers of due dates.

The stars were aligned for me last night, so I fired up the rotavator and ploughed quarter of an eighth of a frosted acre, walking behind the bladed machine, a decidedly peasant variation on nightwalking. There is a whole school of lunar farming, planting by moon phases, the essential principal being that the moon has a pull effect on all water, including the sap in plants; sap rises during the waxing moon and falls towards the roots when it wanes. I do not adhere to lunar plant-ing, but I would not wish to knock it. We are apes who came out of Africa, and less know the questions to ask, let alone have the answers. Anyway, sufficient to say that the moon provided enough light to see by – it was a 'first quarter moon', meaning that the right side of Earth's only natural satellite was wholly lit – and the autumnal frost had crumbled the soil, doing half my job for me. (Like other magical things, such as migrating birds, the frost had arrived in the night.) Before I had fired up the rotavator, I had literally put my ear to the ground: I heard the Pleistocene crackle of nature breaking up the soil, tiny cave by tiny cave. The ploughman's true music, nature herself making tilth, the fine soil needed for a seed bed.

The brilliance of the moonlight on the churned soil behind the rotavator was as wake behind the pro-pellor of a ship.

I was at sea, creating wave-furrows, steering by stars, the moon sailing by.

A pelt-sheened vole fled before me.

My breaths in the dark were a stream of white speech bubbles; the rotavator respired similarly. The sky was pristine and original, and unmarked by aeroplanes, or space junk satellites, the faux shooting stars. Moonlight glinted off the rotavator's cowling as it yawled and pitched. The stone barn beside me was swaddled in black velvet (nights have surprising texture). The world was black and white, and I was Greek.

On reaching the southern end of each row, I faced Orion in the east. Only the Plough is an easier pattern of stars to recognize among the myriad pinpoints of light in the northern night. With a little imagination, Orion is the Hunter, his bow drawn, with the unmistakable three ruler-straight stars Alnitak, Alnilam and Mintaka forming his 'belt'. The stars have always piqued our creativity. Dating back to the eighteenth century BC, the Mesopotamian *Epic of Gilgamesh* pits URU AN-NA (Orion), meaning 'the Light of Heaven', against GUD AN-NA, 'the Bull of Heaven' (Taurus). The Ancient Greeks named Orion for the great handsome hunter of their mythology, chaser of beasts and women alike. Famously, his illicit affair with Eos, the sister of Helios, the sun, accounts for the embarrassed blush of dawn. Orion sought to conquer each of the Pleiades, and to escape his unwanted attention the Seven Sisters were transformed into the constellation which bears their name. (Although, of course, even in the heavens Orion still chases after them; they are to be found by extending a line upwards through Orion's belt and to the right; extending a line through the belt towards the horizon brings you to Sirius, the brightest star in the sky.) On his death, Orion was placed in the sky himself, but appositely for such a procreative figure, there are twin versions of the event. Some tales attest that while hunting on Crete, Orion boasted that he could slay every beast on earth. Gaia, the fountainhead of environmentalism, took understandable umbrage and cracked the earth open, and from a chasm was released an enormous scorpion which duly killed Orion. Or, alternative version: Orion threated to rape one of Artemis' companions, and she summoned the scorpion that stung Orion mortally. You pay your drachma, and you take your pick. Despite his sinning, such were Orion's heroism and manliness – the Greeks, after all, were warrior-agriculturalists – that Zeus placed him in the firmament nonetheless. However, the Hellenic god of gods, never one to forgo the chance of a tragic twist,

stuck the scorpion in the sky as a memorial of what had occurred. To this day, Orion continues to run from the beast that killed him. Thus, Orion descends or 'runs away' as Scorpius rises.

These were the ancient stories above my head as I ploughed with a modern machine, its metal drawbar making straight lines in the soil, much like printed lines in a school exercise book. It was one of those nights when the sky above was a perfect dome, and the stars reached down to the horizon. Every way I looked up there were stars and planets. I contemplated too on the angles and tangents of the constellations, the geometry of the heavens, and my poor geometry on the earth below.

The stars encourage us to look up, and I had seldom seen such a multitude of stars, astronomical grains of ice cast over the sky. They were as plentiful as grains of sand on a beach. I had tried to count them, and in doing so my last furrow lines wobbled and wonked.

'Delirium' has its roots in the Latin for 'going off track when ploughing', entering a non-normal state. An incoherent excitement. Madness. Ulysses was 'delirious' when he took his plough to the beach to try and cultivate there. I had developed 'delirium' in gazing at the stars.

Frost at Midnight

The Frost performs its secret ministry,
Unhelped by any wind. The owlet's cry
Came loud – and hark, again! loud as before.
The inmates of my cottage, all at rest,
Have left me to that solitude, which suits
Abstruser musings: save that at my side
My cradled infant slumbers peacefully.
'Tis calm indeed! so calm, that it disturbs
And vexes meditation with its strange
And extreme silentness. Sea, hill, and wood,
This populous village! Sea, and hill, and wood,
With all the numberless goings-on of life,
Inaudible as dreams! the thin blue flame
Lies on my low-burnt fire, and quivers not;
Only that film, which fluttered on the grate,
Still flutters there, the sole unquiet thing.
Methinks, its motion in this hush of nature
Gives it dim sympathies with me who live,
Making it a companionable form,
Whose puny flaps and freaks the idling Spirit
By its own moods interprets, every where
Echo or mirror seeking of itself,
And makes a toy of Thought.

Samuel Taylor Coleridge

Part V

Slivers of River

AUTUMN, BY THE calendar, and by the smell of decay in the air.

Difficult to not remark the power of the Thames in London, with the original river canalized to create the great watercourse of today which anaconda-coils through the city. Its majesty not lost even in a nocturnal November downpour.

As we walked the towpath from Hammersmith Bridge to Putney, going with the flow, the broad brown water was turbulent, sea-choppy, as if petulantly protesting its imprisoning. The red navigation buoys blipped up and down, sometimes disappearing from view, the river drowning itself in its anguish. We were a family party, the nuclear four, an alteration to my normal mode of solo nightwalking after farm work. There is something original in family nightwalking, a realization that the prehistoric clan still exists under the changeable historical family. When we walk together by night it comes, a little corroded but still alive: a tightening of bonds, for protection. I first noticed this when we started nightwalking *en famille* in the forest near home. If anyone was lost to view among the silent black oaks, there would be calls and refrains, like sheep calling to lambs, and vice versa. Especially this: the two children, Tris and Freda, forging ahead, their senses sharper than those of my wife and myself.

The rain beat off the paving. The reflected lights from Riverside Studios made footbaths of bleach. Runners in uniform yellow high-vis vests loomed out of the rain, and faded away. Cyclists in pink Lycra angrily pinged bells, the spray from their hissing rubber tyres forming an unnatural 90-degree precipitation. Uncurtained windows from chichi apartments, nothing to hide and everything to display, spewed a greasy whiteness on to the river, but not for more than half its width. Across the Thames, the London Wetland Centre lay as a black band of constant calm, a fortress of nature. A dark beacon.

We abandoned the walk, took refuge in the Crab-tree pub. On the brick edge of the path two mallard squatted, looking out over the great river, unperturbed by humans or the elements. Water off a duck's back.

*

As a creature of habit and habitat: the same Thames-side walk, north side, a different autumn night. The tide out, the river low. On the windless smooth water, a last dip of oars, a quietly spoken command. Viking shadows. Other rowers, in the strip-lit boatshed, stowing craft by the aid of hearty laughter. The ceiling above the river the usual London artificial night-time murk, vague and vaguely sci-fi, but definitely not black. The city lost its stars decades ago.

Couples promenading the constructed path. Individuals jogging. An unconsciously agreed low key. From behind the houses the land birds turning off, robin and blackbird, and at the very death of day, a cackling magpie. The last laugh. Down on the sheeny mudbank, trickles of seeping rats. One hopes for a water vole (Kenneth Grahame's 'Ratty' in *The Wind in the Willows*), one gets *Rattus norvegicus*. Some nocturnal terrors remain. In Orwell's *1984* Winston is tortured in Room 101 by putting him in proximity to his greatest fear, the rat.

The rats on the mudbank gather around a dead fish, like ushers around a coffin. An Egyptian goose pokes at some stranded wiggy herbage, in the manner of aged people pecking at food, disbelieving of their reduced circumstances.

Across the water, distinct, the repeated reedy call of coots in the wetland reserve.

From off the water, the must of street dwellers' sleeping bags.

Leigh-on-Sea, 9 p.m. Ten miles down the Thames from Central London as the gull flies, the air of the esplanade smarting with the medicinal tang of saline and the smoke from fags outside the doors of the Crooked Billet. Juvenile herring gulls beg for chips with a teenager's insistent sense of entitlement. Out on the flat estuary, the famous eelgrass beds as black as eels, but each ornamented by the platinum filigree of running seawater in moonlit creeks. The eelgrass is catnip for brent geese, a small, dark fowl – 'brent' is a corruption of the Old Norse *brantr*, 'burnt' – that is the most northerly breeding goose in the world, breeding on the tundra of the Arctic Circle. Of the 300,000 brent worldwide, 4,000 come to Leigh-on-Mudflat. Rather more than Borth.

Leaning against the railings. Waiting. Pint in hand. Supping. The hint of first star points in the mustered dusk above the estuary. The air charged with expectancy, soon satisfied. Low, yapping like dogs, advance bands of brents swing in from the sea. They come in tight family groups, one after another, always in a parade V formation. (The shape helps the flock to make better progress; birds in V formation can fly 70 per cent further than one bird flying alone.) In the air-brake whoosh of landing the birds are near invisible against the mud, except for the stroboscopic flash of white from their hundred beating wing-bars.

The smokers have joined us, everyone exclaiming about the geese; someone says to me, 'This is just the start, there'll be clouds of them later.' Clink of glasses. More chat about Leigh-on-Mudflat's pride and joy, the eelgrass beds and their brent geese. Then, carried on a gust, the sound of the brent geese talking to each other in the moonlight. Their language as familiar as it is foreign.

Midsummer in the city, about 10 p.m., folks being witty. Coming out of Hammersmith Underground I pass a gang of youths, joshing, drinking lager from cans; one pours the contents over the head of his mate. Shampoo!

The heat is on. Police sirens scream – a city catch-phrase. After an afternoon inside a library, I've opted for the familiar walk when 'in town', Hammersmith to Putney Bridge, but on the south side.

Outside St Paul's Church a fox slinks through the metal railings; the gaps between them are perhaps four inches in extent. A rural fox would get stuck. From across the road, through the uriney light of the street-lamps, a muscled guy in a black singlet shouts, 'Foxy!', boom-box voice audible even over the traffic from the flyover almost above our heads.

I feel like a country fox myself. Out of place. People fear the night in woods, nyctohylophobia (conjoined from the Greek 'nycto', night, and 'hyle', forest, with 'phobos', fear). I'm fritted by the city at night, its people, its people with rules and mores I do not always understand.

London, of course, never gets truly dark, which is part of its estranging. It never achieves the rural, thick blackness that is a type of nothingness, a type of perfection. The streetlamps are too strong, and tonight the bloated moon is their useful unwitting aid. The city is stuck in a perpetual purgatorial twilight; the growling car-lights on the flyover diffuse rather than beam. Contra the sultriness there's a 'vibe' to the night, edgy, adrenalined. We're dancing before the fall.

Crossing over Hammersmith Bridge, newly pedestrianized (it has micro-structural issues) but of Victorian vintage: an engineering work of imported imperial exotic, complete with minarets. A suspended Shangri-La cast in iron, painted green, tricked out in gold. In the demi-light the bridge floats dreamily over the wide, high-tide river. And to cross it is to effect a transition from one sort of nightwalk to another. Whereas the parallel north-bank walk is hard brick and angles and Fulham Palace football ground, the south-bank Thames Path, reached by just a hard left turn on exiting the bridge, is a walk on the wild side. One stumbles on the evidence immediately: the south path is uneven, gravelled. This natural satisfaction underfoot, the path becomes a narrow tunnel through trees. Oak, ash, sycamore, alder, and poplars, some with gigantic horizontal limbs to hold the roof of the black tunnel up. And black it is, since the bank for hundreds of yards is unlit. I avow that the Thames Path here is as dark as London gets. Yet, from the swarthy bankside vegetation, white flowers of bind-weed elven-trumpet the way.

I'm going with the flow, downstream, the great river low and to my left, rarely meeting obstacles, just the occasional puffing head-torched jogger, and one impatient bell-ringing Deliveroo cyclist with three front lamps. On the river, a swan up-ending carelessly; on the bank, a heron entranced by the sliding water; squatting low in some indefinable tree, a cormorant, vulture-mean aura and the dazzle of the electric other bank in its eyes; perching in an oak, a robin singing; in the summer city, the birds work late. Where the tunnel of trees opens, the pattern of the branches against

107

the sky makes ceiling panels of painterly styles. Clotty oak is *fête galante*, Watteau and naiads.

The night gives permission to fancy. And as well as phantasy, the night permits the lesser senses. They are always there under modern human, *Homo librarius officus*, and given opportunity they come, a little benumbed maybe, but they come. Night reveals the alertness of original Adam and Eve. In the city I am wary – of my fellow humans. In this heightened nocturnal state, such is my acuteness of hearing I can hear the padding footsteps of unseen Canada geese on brown mud, the suspicion of a breeze in the tops of the poplar towers. From the bankside vegetation, the gleamy river itself, comes a sequence of scents: sniff of salt (the Thames being tidal here); pondy-reedy, wet-dog core; cow parsley spiciness; nettly sour acid – and a definite beeriness. The whiff arrives in waves. I keep looking around the dark corridor for secret drinkers, then understand that the beeriness is the fermenting combination of all the midsummer scents, and it is old and original. A Neanderthal standing on the bank of the river, spear in hand, would have known it.

I mention some of these things because I did exactly the same walk in the afternoon, when I was guided by sight. And failed to notice them.

Night Notes: Moon Names

I've cut the corn by the light of the harvest moon, and I've walked around the garden on the scented spring night of the pink moon. I've watched the fox prowl under the wolf moon, and often under a cold moon, I've dispensed hay to snow-chested sheep. Once, in the sort of strange synchronicity that happens only once in a blue moon, I was driving through a flood when Creedence Clearwater Revival's 'Bad Moon Rising' came on the radio.

Our modern Western method of measuring time, the Gregorian calendar, is derived from the solar cycle of the year, but for other cultures the moon was determinant. The clarity of the moon's phases – the waxing and waning, the full moon every twenty-nine and a half days – made the lunar cycle a convenient calendar for other old cultures, such as Celtic, Anglo-Saxon and Native American.

Full-moon names are syntheses of utility and poetry. Take 'harvest moon', the full moon that happens closest to the autumnal equinox. For several nights in a row, a full moon rises just after sunset, and hangs fat and round and white in the sky. Before headlights on combine harvesters, farmers took advantage of this natural floodlight to extend the scything of the crop, hence, technically, why it's called a harvest moon. But 'harvest moon' is a phrase full of fecundity, the chattering echo of Hardy's labouring wights, moonshine on glinting steel, hares loping through stubble.

Full-moon names are confirmations of the workings of the heavens – because as surely as the sun does rise, the full moon does shine – and of the traditional countryside ways. The 'hay moon' was July's full moon, when the meadow was cut, and the brilliance of the 'hunter's moon' of October was the sign for the family to prepare for winter, for father and son to shoot game for the larder, for the cottage fire to be stoked, for the poacher's haunch of venison to be hung in the chimney for smoking.

The full-moon names, they memorialize too the natural calendar. The cruel coming of winter earned December's full moon the name 'cold moon'. January's 'wolf moon' was named by the Celts for wolves howling the lack of food in midwinter. (A sage people, the Celts also named the same month's full moon 'stay home moon'.) The last full moon of winter in March is the 'death moon' in Old English. Happier, the 'pink moon' of America's April notes the blossoming of ground phlox, and elsewhere a general sense of springtime rebirth, hence 'egg moon' in Anglo-Saxon.

May's full moon is known in many countries as the 'flower moon'. Across the Atlantic July's warm full moon is a 'buck moon', recognizing the shedding of antlers by male deer. They say tomayto, we say tomato. However, little in the British experience prepares one for Americans calling August's full moon 'sturgeon moon', after the profusion of this 200lb fossil fish in the Great Lakes. Our Anglo-Saxon forbears settled for the discreet 'grain moon'. With the 're-wilding' of Britain with beavers we are able to join those state-side in referring to November's full moon as 'beaver moon'. Another name for the month's full moon is the meteorologically accurate 'frost moon'.

The only disappointment in the naming of full moons is 'blue moon', despite the famous Sinatra song of loneliness and one true love. A blue moon is, frankly, a quite commonplace phenomenon. The moon completes twelve full cycles of its phases in about 354 days – which is eleven days short of a calendar year. Every two and a half years or so the difference adds up to an extra, thirteenth, full moon occurring during the year and this occurrence is a . . . blue moon.

A 'supermoon' occurs when Earth's only satellite orbits exceptionally close to us – say, a mere 223,301 miles – while showing its full white face; a supermoon exceeds the brightness of an average-sized full moon by some 16 per cent. Tides may be higher too. Certainly, the world at night will be swathed in romantic light, and we shall be struck in awe and wonder at supernature.

Part VI

Wolf Moon

THE FIRST FULL moon of the year. The wolf moon. To take the dog for a nocturnal ramble was a poetic irresistibility.

Humans are diurnal beings, and stepping outside into the dark is never neutral. Some feeling, on a range from fear to exaltation, is always engendered. Tonight, it was disbelief. Stepping on to the farm lane, the great white orb ahead, I could have read by its light a small print book, and its rays transmogrified the black Labrador into a golden one.

On the wall by the barn a tawny owl regarded our approach, until something more interesting arrested its attention in the orchard behind. With a mechanical swivel, as if pivoted, Old Brown turned his head 180 degrees. (There are owls that can rotate their heads through 270 degrees.) The tawny flew off, a leaf blown by the wind, a scene from a silent film.

Frost was already taking grip; on the grass strip in

the middle of the lane my boots shushed a metronomic
lullaby to aid the sleeping land. The poor pigeons
were unimpressed. Our perambulation disturbed their
roosting, and they clappered out of the lane's hem-
ming trees in bow waves as we progressed. There was
the click of claws and the snuffling nose of the dog,
otherwise quiet, as though the white moon-bleach
had imposed a frozen silence on the fields and woods.
Full moonshine tends to smother star- and planet-
spotting, but Mars was conspicuous in its attendance
of the moon, a gentleman equerry, a man-in-waiting.

Mars, the red planet. We invariably depict the
celestial bodies as white, but the heavens are coloured.
The constellation Orion boasts the orange Betelgeuse
and the blue Rigel. Dubhe in the Plough is yellow.
Venus is golden. Sirius, the dog star, even twinkles in
varying hues.

In the wood on the hill the cold brilliance of the
moonlight cast the shadows of the bare oak branches
in such sooty blackness that they appeared as cracks in
the geology of the ground. Natural crazy paving. Or a
scraperboard picture.

Walking at night is an exercise in translation,
rationality into imagination, and vice versa. Duo
lingo. Animated by my imagination a dead hazel tree
clad with ivy became a rearing unicorn; the umbra

of the grey wolf pawing a football on the verge was revealed to be a red fox pawing a hedgehog. The Labrador's sense of scent was quicker than my eyesight, and she decided on the chase before I could issue a command. However, a fox can manage 31mph, and a portly Labrador rather less; she made just twenty yards along the deer path before returning on the command. (Once again defeated in the hunt, she will essay again, since it is her nature, just as it the nature of the moon to rise each evening.) Sulphurous and acidic, like lemon on the turn, the lingering *eau sauvage* of the fox was thick enough to choke on. Indubitably, foxes stink. You know this on a winter's night when creeping frost locks down all the usual smells of the earth, and Renard walks kingly on an olfactory *tabula rasa*. Territory, such as the deer path, is staked by scenting, the primary scent being composed of urine laced with the compound isopentyl methyl sulphide. Another odour is made by the violet gland near the base of the vulpine tail, so called because the emission possesses a floral aspect; foxes waft this smell around with their fluffy tail. There are also scent-producing glands in the skin between the toes and footpads, and it is the telltale secretions from these which hounds pick up on the hunt. The emissions of the fox may be noisome to us; its fellows make sense of the scents, containing as they do lonely-heart adverts and trespassers-beware notices. Chemistry as communication.

The deer path runs through coppiced hazels, cut off at the base to produce many trunks, skyward-seeking fingers of a buried hand. The works of man become works of nature; every one of the trunks was plastered with patches of moon-affinity lichen. The trees of winter may net stars, or hang them from their branches as baubles, and consequently preserve the wood's shadowy secrets. The trees were no match for the wolf moon, though, which was as illuminating as a searchlight. Since we were on the deer path, I decided to follow it down to the brook. Lunar-powered, the lichens on the hazel paparazzi-camera-flashed at us.

There was a view down the passageway path to the other side of the valley, where a single car crawled up the hill, its beam splashing the hedges in white. Traffic during the day is mundane, all school runs, shopping and commuting. Cars at night carry stories of assignations and voyages.

On a nightwalk the mind itself wanders. The night is a parallel dimension. Alone in the landscape – for hardly anyone nightwalks – the liberation from the pettifogging details of daily life, such as the shopping list and school pick-up, is intoxicating. You will never be so free as you are at night under the moon and stars. You could drown in the delight of it.

Quite solipsistic, nightwalking. An exercise in ego. A sequence of ontological propositions. *Solvitur ambulando*. The Latin for 'It is solved by walking.' When afoot thoughts emerge spontaneously, effortlessly, like water from a hillside spring. Aristotle did his thinking and lecturing while walking, and students of his school of philosophy in Athens became known as the Peripatetic philosophers – those 'given to walking about'. Jean-Jacques Rousseau confessed, 'I can only meditate when I am walking. When I stop, I cease to think; my mind only works with my legs.' If classical philosophers did not nightwalk, they should have done. *Optimum solvitur nocte ambulando*. Of course, a loser in the betting shop cares little for moonlight nuance.

Pontificating so, I almost stepped in the badger latrine, a squarish hole about a foot in length in long grass, and heaped with black droppings which glistened in the moonlight. There was a slight chemical smell to the loo, which prompted the fleeting notion of Mr and Mrs Badger using lavatory disinfectant. A badger dung pit cannot be mistaken for anything else; Brock is the only British animal to construct and use an open privy. In a quaint mind frame, *Meles meles* possesses a charmingly human sense of tidiness, celebratedly

119

'spring cleaning' the sett by removing old bedding, as well as the pit toiletry. Base science declares the latrine a territorial marker of powerful pungency, and sett cleaning paltry self-serving hygiene.

The deer path runs to the brook in the flat base of the valley for the good reason that deer drink. On reaching the edge of the wood I could see, across the furrowed field, three roe deer lapping at the silver stream. We halted. I had no wish to disturb them; the night belongs to the animals. I am simply a chance interloper.

I tried for the demeanour of a tree, and signalled with a finger for the dog to sit. A canine stump. Such was the stillness in the small moonlit valley that it appeared as a scene etched on frosted glass, and as fragile.

The deer ambled off upstream to become lost behind the brambly scrub of the far bank, leaving the dog and I to cautiously make our way down around the edge of the field to the water. The brook was near full, and as the dog and I promenaded along its edge it played its music, in sequences, as in the bars of a musical score: stretches of silken quiet; crescendo over the fallen alder trunk; some tuneful gurgling in the narrows; *boo-be-de-boo* on the bends.

The brook runs in an almost straight line, and the

moonlight lay along it, in precise correspondence. By day the brook had been disagreeable khaki; lunar light alchemized it into a reflective stream of mercury. In the water musick were stored sounds of the past: the clash of steel from ancient battles, the folk songs of labourers when a-haying, wolves crying at the moon. Water at night has memory.

They say you never step into the same stream twice. By the same law of time no nightwalk is the same as the last. Two nights ago I stood in this same spot and the moon had been unable to pierce the cloud, and was no more than an eye, with boiled white pupil and iridescent iris of some alien sky whale. Last night the moon shone thrillingly on mist, lighting every particle, creating the dreamy dazzling haze that one imagines is the transport to the afterlife. Tomorrow the moon will commence waning, a misshapen melting lacking dignity.

But tonight, in atmospheric conditions of pure, cold clarity, the wolf moon was in its pomp. If the full moon diminished the stars, it failed to obliterate them. Sirius twinkled in the pentagram rays of a kid's idea of a star.

In years of nightwalking I have learned the major constellations. The second-century astron-omer Ptolemy defined forty-eight constellations; the

International Astronomical Union now recognizes eighty-eight. But a constellation is an arbitrary categorization, with its stars not necessarily related to others in the grouping. The designation 'constellation' is merely the feeble pinky-grey cells of humans imposing an order on the universe that it does not really have. To join the dots of the stars to fashion one's own constellation is equally amusement and affirmation. A DIY narrative available to everyone.

Tonight, I squinted at the stars around Orion in Quadrant NQ1 and saw a wolf's head, with a gleaming canine in its open, ravening mouth.

In the wood the fox started howling.

Mon in the Mone

(The Man in the Moon)

Mon in the mone stond ant strit;
On is bot-forke is burthen he bereth.
Hit is muche wonder that he nadoun slyt;
For doute leste he valle, he shoddreth ant shereth.
When the forst freseth, muche chele he byd.
The thornes beth kene, is hattren totereth.
Nis no wytht in the world that wot wen he syt,
Ne, bote hit bue the hegge, whet wedes he wereth.

Whider trowe this mon ha the wey take?
He hath set is o fot is other toforen;
For non hithte that he hath, ne sytht me hym ner shake.
He is the sloweste mon that ever wes yboren!
Wher he were o the feld pycchynde stake,
For hope of ys thornes to dutten is doren,
He mot myd is twybyl other trous make,
Other al is dayes werk ther were yloren.

This ilke mon upon heh, when-er he were,
Wher he were y the mone boren ant yfed,
He leneth on is forke ase a grey frere;
This crokede caynard, sore he is adred!

124

Hit is mony day go that he was here;
Ichot of is ernde he nath nout ysped.
He hath hewe sumwher a burthen of brere;
Tharefore sum hayward hath taken ys wed.

Yef thy wed ys ytake, bring hom the trous!
Sete forth thyn other fot! Stryd over sty!
We shule preye the haywart hom to ur hous,
Ant maken hym at heyse, for the maystry,
Drynke to hym deorly of fol god bous,
Ant oure dame douse shal sitten hym by.
When that he is dronke ase a dreynt mous,
Thenne we schule borewe the wed ate bayly.

This mon hereth me nout, thah Ich to hym crye!
Ichot the cherl is def! The Del hym todrawe!
Thah Ich yeye upon heth, nulle nout hye;
The lostlase ladde con nout o lawe.
Hupe forth, Hubert, hosede pye!
Ichot thart amarscled into the mawe!
Thah me teone with hym that myn teh mye,
The cherld nul nout adoun er the day dawe!

Anonymous*

* From the 1300s, taken from the Complete Harley 2253
Manuscript.

NIGHT TRACKS

Nocturnes for Nature-lovers

The title Nocturne aptly applies to the pieces so named by [John] Field, for it bears our thoughts at the outset toward those hours wherein the soul, released from all the cares of the day, is lost in self-contemplation, and soars toward the regions of a starlit heaven.

Franz Liszt on Irish composer John Field, the first person to title instrumental works 'nocturnes', 1869

J. S. Bach, 'The Goldberg Variations', 1741

Samuel Barber, Nocturne, Op. 33 ('Homage to John Field'), 1959

Béla Bartók, *Out of Doors* (IV, 'The Night's Music'), 1926

Ludwig van Beethoven, Piano Sonata No. 14 in C sharp minor, Op. 27 ('Moonlight Sonata'), 1801

Frédéric Chopin, Nocturne in G major, Op. 37, No. 2, 1839

—Nocturne in E flat major, Op. 9, No. 2, 1832 ['I'm working on a Nocturne that I hope will be better than any that I've written. It's a kind of reverie in the moonlight on a beautiful spring evening.']

Carl Czerny, *Huit Nocturnes*, Op. 368, *c.* 1840

Claude Debussy, 'Clair de Lune', 1905

—*Trois Nocturnes*, 1899

—'Réverie', 1897–9

Gabriel Fauré, *Les 13 Nocturnes*, *c.* 1875–1921

John Field, Nocturne for piano No. 6 in F major ('Cradle Song'), 1817

—Nocturne for piano No. 7 in C major ('Reverie'), 1821

Aram Khachaturian, *Masquerade* (II, 'Nocturne'), 1944

Franz Liszt, Nocturne for piano in B major ('En rêve'), 1885

Gustav Mahler, 'Um Mitternacht', from *Rückert-Lieder*, 1901

Wolfgang Amadeus Mozart, Serenade for strings No. 13 in G major ('Eine kleine Nachtmusik'), 1787

Sergei Prokofiev, *Cinderella*, Op. 87, Act 2: No. 38 ('Midnight'), 1940–44

Henry Purcell, Nunc dimittis in B flat major, before 1682

Camille Saint-Saëns, 'Calme des nuits', Op. 68, No. 1, 1882

Arnold Schoenberg, 'Verklärte Nacht', Op. 4, 1899

Clara Schumann, Nocturne in F major, Op. 6, No. 2, 1836

Robert Schumann: Romance No. 2 in F sharp major, Op. 28, 1839

Alexander Scriabin, Two Nocturnes, Op. 5, 1890

The Moth Garden

Thus hath the candle singed the moth.
O these deliberate fools!
When they do choose,
They have the wisdom by their wit to lose.

Portia, *The Merchant of Venice*,
William Shakespeare

FEW PEOPLE FIND moths as enchanting as their day-time relatives. Their cause is not helped by their habit of eating clothes. Or fluttering around a lighted window which, like Shakespeare's candle, they likely confuse with the moon. Or, indeed, the profusion of moth species – over 2,500 in the UK – which can make identifying individual species irritatingly tricky. Yet they are so much more interesting than butterflies, whose life is but a flashy, prancy hour of superficial delight. Moths touch primal fears – the sight of a ghost moth hovering over a meadow in moonlight will unnerve even an empiricist, and the death's-head hawk-moth is a cultural symbol of doom, from Thomas Hardy's *The Return of the Native* to Thomas Harris's *The Silence of the Lambs*, via Pre-Raphaelite artist William Holman Hunt's *The Hireling Shepherd*. Understandably. The death's-head hawk-moth is so named because the markings on its thorax resemble a skull. The scientific name, *Acherontia atropos*, is little comfort, Atropos being the third of the Greek Fates (the one who snipped the thread of life with her scissors) and Acheron the River of Woe in the Greek Underworld. The whopping four-inch-long caterpillar, usually a fetching shade of banana, feeds on potato leaves.

Moths slough off our casual stereotyping, our crude classifications of nature. Moths are the thinking person's, the soul person's Lepidoptera. Emissaries from the Other. Some moths are indeed plain, pre-ball Cinderellas, but drabness is evolutionary perfection to escape detection; in the case of the lappet moth, its wings are the exact colour of withered bramble leaves, enabling the insect to lie up during the day unremarked by predators. So much for the unremarked: the adult elephant hawk-moth, pretty in

velveteen pink and gold, is a Disney princess's idea of . . . a butterfly. Equally rococo, the garden tiger moth is a seventies fashion crime of spotted orange hindwings under snow leopard forewings. It also happens to be determinedly diurnal, thus one of the 130 or so breeds of British moths that break the rule that 'moths fly by night and butterflies by day'. Moths, they provoke the mind.

Moths evolved before butterflies. Touch the delicate wings of a fallen moth, its glittery dust on your fingertip, and you touch 200 million years of time. You touch a creature that knew the dinosaurs.

Moths. They come in a nearly numberless variety of appearance. They come as a snow blizzard of micro-moths, speck-small, an eighth of an inch, in the car headlights on the lane, and they come as burnished brass (*Diachrysia chrysitis*), which due to light-reflecting scales does truly shine as bold as burnished brass. (The pearlescent sheen is due to the arrangement of wing scales rather than pigment.) They come too trailing names of such poetry: garden tiger, gold swift, map-winged swift, small angle shades, double-striped pug, larger Welsh wave, orange underwing and autumn green carpet.

Above all, moths are a vital part of the night-time food chain for bats, spiders, owls and mammals. Daytime predators, especially small perching birds, eat sleeping moths if they uncover them along with their caterpillar offspring.

Many moths are excellent plant pollinators.

Moths. They deserve – and need – a place in the garden.

To invite moths into the garden, plant night-flowering, nectar-rich plants, many of which have specifically evolved to attract nocturnal insects. Most 'moth flowers' are white or pale-coloured, so that moths can see them at dusk. An 'ordinary' urban garden attracts around a hundred moth species over the year. A moth-friendly urban garden should easily attract 250 moth species a year. A balcony garden will be a smorgasbord for moths.

A moth garden will also be a fragrant retreat for you. Shangri-La at home. Let the night in.

Ten Plants for Moths

Evening primrose (*Oenothera spp.*) – Flowers remain closed during the day, then uncurl at dusk.

Tobacco plant (*Nicotiana affinis*) – This flowering tobacco plant is sweetly scented and blandishment for moths. The luminous white salver-shaped flowers grow up to 9 centimetres (3.5 inches) long in the summer. Prefers fertile, moist but well-drained soil in sun or partial shade. A biennial, easily grown from seed.

Night-scented stock (*Matthiola bicornis*) – A guaranteed lure for moths. Not good on acid soils.

Buddleia (*Buddleja davidii*) 'White Profusion' – A luminous, white variety of buddleia with fragrant flowers. Hugely attractive to moths.

Bluebeard (*Caryopteris x clandonensis*) – A shrub whose blue flowers glow in moonlight.

Giant sea holly (*Eryngium giganteum*) 'Silver Ghost' – A showy plant, which grows up to 90 centimetres high and produces silvery-white metallic heads in its second year.

Hebe (*Plantaginaceae*) 'Great Orme' – Produces spikes of pink-white flowers in summer/autumn.

Honeysuckle (*Lonicera spp.*) – There are about 180 species of honeysuckle, all magnets for moths. The *L. Caprifolium* is guaranteed to bloom early – mid-May is the usual date – and the flowers are creamy white when they first open, and deepen to pink as they age. It climbs to 3 metres. Unfussy and easy to grow.

Jasmine (*Jasminum officinale*) – A white-flowering jasmine.

Bell heather (*Erica cinerea*) – Produces honey scent from pink flowers.

Also consider: night-flowering catchfly (*Silene nocti-flora*); pinks (*Dianthus* species, especially *D. plumarius*); bladder campion (*Silene vulgaris*); sweet williams (*D. barbatus*) – but only the single-flowered, old-fashioned, cottage-garden kind.

One daytime moth to look out for is the hummingbird hawk-moth, which hovers in front of flowers as it sucks out nectar through its long thin tongue. It is a migrant to southern Britain in warm summers.

To provide for the caterpillars of moths, leave knapweeds, long grass and thistles in wilder corners of the garden. Lady's bedstraw is food for the extraordinary elephant hawk-moth caterpillar. Native trees and hedging plants, such as birch, oak, willow and hawthorn, host many moth caterpillars.

ENVOI

Good-Night

The skylarks are far behind that sang over the down;
I can hear no more those suburb nightingales;
Thrushes and blackbirds sing in the gardens of the town
In vain: the noise of man, beast, and machine prevails.

But the call of children in the unfamiliar streets
That echo with a familiar twilight echoing,
Sweet as the voice of nightingale or lark, completes
A magic of strange welcome, so that I seem a king

Among men, beast, machine, bird, child, and the ghost
That in the echo lives and with the echo dies.
The friendless town is friendly; homeless, I am not lost;
Though I know none of these doors, and meet but
    strangers' eyes.

Never again, perhaps, after to-morrow, shall
I see these homely streets, these church windows alight,
Not a man or woman or child among them all:
But it is All Friends' Night, a traveller's good-night.

Edward Thomas

ACKNOWLEDGEMENTS

There are stars to be found outside Heaven. So, to the following stellar people, my gratitude: Penny Lewis-Stempel, as always, for ideas, inspiration, and more than a little textual improvement; at the Soho Agency, Julian Alexander, Sarah Stamp, and Annette Murphy; and at Transworld, Susannah Wadeson, Sharika Teelwah, Beci Kelly, Kate Samano.

CREDITS

Alamy: *The Darkening Sky of the First Night* (p. 9), illustration by Gustav Doré, 1860 for Dante's *The Divine Comedy*. PhotoStock-Israel/Alamy stock photo; badger (p. 22), 19th era/Alamy stock photo; **Rob Barnes**: *Flight Over the Barley* (p.53); **Bridge-man Images**: *The Moon* (p. 15), 1860; **Getty Images**: Meteor shower as observed by Andrew Ellicott (p. 19), eighteenth century, Universal History Archive/Getty Images; Orion constellation (p. 96), mikromanó/Getty Images; **Indianapolis Museum of Art Collection, Newfields**: *Nocturne: The Thames at Battersea* (p. 99) by James A. Whistler, 1878, gift in memory of Kurt F. Pantzer, Sr; **Library of Congress**: Lunar halo and luminescent cross [detail of the balloon Zénith's long-distance flight from Paris to Arcachon (p. 17), March 1875; **Metropolitan Museum of Art, New York**: Tiger Moth card from the *Butterflies and Moths of America* series (p. 135), published by Louis Prang & Co., 1862–9, the Jefferson R. Burdick Collection, gift of Jefferson R. Burdick; **National Gallery of Art, Washington**: *Moonlit River Landscape* (p. viii), detail of engraving by Schelte Adams Bolswert (1586–1659), after Sir Peter Paul Rubens (1577–1640), Ailsa Mellon Bruce Fund; *Deer in the Woods (Les cerfs sous bois)* (p. 121), etching by Charles-François Daubigny, 1850, Rosenwald Collection; *Nightingale in a Bush* (p. 72), etching by Jacques Callot, 1628, R. L. Baumfeld Collection; **Howard Phipps**: *Boxing Hares* (p. 5), wood engraving; **Sue Scullard**: *Barn Owl* (p. 13), wood engraving; **Smithsonian Libraries and Archives**: *Rhinolophus* Pearsonii (p. 46) from *Anatomical and Zoological Researches* ... by John Anderson, 1878; **Wellcome Collection**: Shepherd boy resting under a tree (p. 63); A Nightjar (p. 61) 1889; Constellations of Ursa major and Ursa minor (p. 91), 1808; The Death's-Head Hawk Moth (p. 133) from *Butterflies and Moths (British)* by William S. Furneaux, 1894; **Art Werger**: *Rising Tide* (p. 79), ed. 40. Mezzotint, 2015; **Yale Center for British Art**: *Study of a Clouded Moonlit Sky* (p. 31), undated wash painting by George Romney (1734–1802), Paul Mellon Collection; *The Harvest Moon* (p. 113), oil painting by Samuel Palmer, *c.*1833, Paul Mellon Collection.

If you enjoyed *Night Life*, you will love these previous books from John Lewis-Stempel:

THE SECRET LIFE OF THE OWL

There is something about owls. They are creatures of the night, and thus of magic. But – with the sapient flatness of their faces, their big, round eyes, their paternal expressions – they are also reassuringly familiar. We see them as wise, like Athena's owl, and loyal, like Hedwig. Here, John Lewis-Stempel explores the legends and history of the owl. And in vivid, lyrical prose, he celebrates all the realities of this magnificent creature, whose natural powers are as fantastic as any myth.

THE GLORIOUS LIFE OF THE OAK

The oak is our most beloved and most familiar tree. For centuries, oak touched every part of a Briton's life – from cradle to coffin. It was oak that made the 'wooden walls' of Nelson's navy, and the navy that allowed Britain to rule the world. John Lewis-Stempel explores our long relationship with this iconic tree and retells oak stories from folklore, myth and legend – oaks bearing the souls of the dead, the Green Man, and fertility rites on Oak Apple Day. Of all the trees, it is the oak that speaks most clearly to us.

THE PRIVATE LIFE OF THE HARE

The hare is a rare sight for most people. We know them only from legends and stories. They are shape-shifters, witches' familiars and symbols of fertility. They are arrogant, as in Aesop's 'The Hare and the Tortoise', and absurd, as in Lewis Carroll's Mad March Hare. In the absence of observed facts, speculation and fantasy have flourished. But real hares? What are they like? In elegant prose John Lewis-Stempel celebrates how, in an age when television cameras have revealed so much in our landscape, the hare remains as elusive and magical as ever.

THE WILD LIFE OF THE FOX

The fox is our apex predator, our most beautiful and clever killer. We have witnessed its wild touch, watched it slink by bins at night and been chilled by its high-pitched scream. And yet we long to stroke the tumbling cubs outside their tunnel homes and watch the vixen stalk the cornfield. Foxes captivate us like no other species. Exploring a long and sometimes complicated relationship, *The Wild Life of the Fox* captures our love – and sometimes loathing – of this magnificent creature in vivid detail and lyrical prose.

THE SOARING LIFE OF THE LARK

Skylarks are the heralds of our countryside. Their music is the quintessential sound of spring. The spirit of English pastoralism, they inspire poets, composers and farmers alike. In the trenches of World War One they were a reminder of the chattering meadows of home. We watch as they climb the sky, delight in their joyful singing, and yet we harm them, too. *The Soaring Life of the Lark* explores the music and poetry, the breathtaking heights and the struggle to survive of one of Britain's most iconic songbirds.

NIGHTWALKING

As the human world settles down each evening, nocturnal animals prepare to take back the countryside. Taking readers on four walks through the four seasons, John Lewis-Stempel reveals a world bursting with life and normally hidden from view. Out beyond the cities, it is still possible to see the night sky full of stars, or witness a moonbow, an arch of white light in the heavens. It is time for us to leave our lairs and go tramping. To join our fellow creatures of the night.

THE CURIOUS LIFE OF THE CUCKOO

Early nature writers, regarding the cuckoo in God's design, could make no sense of *Cuculus canorus* at all. Mad or bad, few birds have attracted as much folklore, myth, music and literary allusion as the cuckoo. In *The Curious Life of the Cuckoo*, John Lewis-Stempel delves into the bird's unique biology and its captivating role in our cultural imagination, turning his exquisite prose to one of the strangest tales of the countryside.

John Lewis-Stempel is the only person to have won the Wainwright Prize for Nature Writing twice, with *Meadowland* and *Where Poppies Blow*. His other books include the *Sunday Times* bestsellers *The Running Hare*, *The Wood* and *Woodston*, and most recently *England: A Natural History*. He is a former Magazine Columnist of the Year. He writes about nature for *Country Life* and *The Times*, and farms sheep. Traditionally.